MOTHER
and the TIGER
A Memoir of the Killing Fields

DANA HUI LIM

ODYSSEY
BOOKS

Published by Odyssey Books in 2013
ISBN 978-1-922200-10-5

www.odysseybooks.com.au

A Cataloguing-in-Publication entry is available from the
National Library of Australia

ISBN: 978-1-922200-10-5 (pbk)
ISBN: 978-1-922200-11-2 (ebook)

For Bouy

Author's Note

My story began as a jumbled collection of early memories. Events and images floated in and out of my mind as faces and places were recalled: some vivid and sharp, others dim and almost forgotten. I have tried to sort through these glimpses of my past so that they flow together into a coherent timeline. With encouragement from my loved ones I have found it therapeutic and rewarding to write about my experiences under the Khmer Rouge regime. I have always had a fear of confronting the past. There was a possibility that dredging up old terrors would have a negative effect on what is now a happy and fulfilling life.

There are millions of Cambodian people suffering from the emotional and psychological trauma inflicted by years of conflict and repression. Most of them cope with no psychological support. To protect myself I tried hard not to think about what had happened for a long time. I avoided anything that might remind me of the Khmer Rouge, and I lost my trust in people. The trauma had damaged my ability to relate to others socially and I doubted that I would ever completely trust anyone or anything again. Thirty years later, the experiences of the Cambodian people during that time still represent their most important and long lasting memories. Most people lost at least one family member, usually in horrific circumstances. This legacy of loss has never been dealt with properly, and in fact Cambodian culture does not permit people to openly talk about their emotions outside the family and little enough within it. Distress, grief and pain are buried deeply and the bearer assumes a mask of composure. As a result, problems go untreated because any medical diagnosis of mental illness, no matter how legitimate, would bring humiliation.

The past is something that I had tried to leave on the road behind me. Most of my mental scars were well hidden for a long time, set aside in my battle first for survival, then for academic success and financial security. I never needed to watch war movies to gain an understanding of what people had suffered in the past, for I had lived through it myself. All I needed to do was to close my eyes and my own wartime experiences and memories would come back uninvited: the horror, the screams and the stench. In these memoirs I have tried to use words to exorcise the past, and in doing so, healing myself.

I was able to recognise the sounds of war by the age of two, when the spread of the Vietnamese conflict began to intrude into my homeland. B-52 bombers from the United States made at least 3500 secret bombing raids over Cambodia in a fourteen-month period beginning in March 1969. Of course it was no secret to us. The sound and effect of a 1000-pound bomb was unmistakable.

My hometown of Kratie was one of the first areas to fall to Khmer Rouge control in the summer of 1973. The 'liberation' would not have occurred without the US economic and military destabilisation of Cambodia. The rise of the Khmer Rouge began in 1966 after the American escalation in Vietnam. It peaked in 1969–73 after the carpet-bombing of Cambodia's countryside by American B-52s. This was probably the single most important factor in the Khmer Rouge's takeover.

At the age of six I was forced from the family home that my

parents had spent their life savings to build. We left Kratie city in north-eastern Cambodia and were sent to work in labour camps, along with thousands of other children who had been separated from their parents and siblings by the Khmer Rouge. *Angkar,* the Cambodian name of the new regime, became our father and mother.

From April 1975 until January 1979, the Khmer Rouge communists targeted what they saw as bourgeoisie principles by killing Cambodia's educated people, anyone they perceived as a threat, and indeed anyone at all if it served as an example. Intellectuals, the ethnic Chinese, the ethnic Vietnamese and anyone thought to be influential, such as actors, singers and leaders were targeted. Soldiers were sent to hunt down and execute these people and their families. They obliterated all infrastructure and education, seeking to reset the country to 'Year Zero'. They wanted to create a society in which people lived off the land in a farming utopia that mimicked a pastoral ideal that had never actually existed. It was meant to be the glorious beginning of a new nation that could apparently only be achieved after the murder of two million people, approximately one quarter of the country's population. This was accomplished through starvation, forced labour, execution, disease and occasionally suicide.

For four years the freedom of the press, of movement, worship, organisation, association and discussion utterly disappeared. The whole nation was kidnapped and then besieged from within. The borders were closed, foreign embassies and press agencies expelled, newspapers and television stations shut down, radios confiscated, mail and telephone use suppressed. Opposition of any kind was met with brutal death.

I am just one of thousands of sons and daughters of the killing fields. War is inevitable when insane leaders are permitted to take power, and when those who could make a difference choose to look the other way. I would like to share my story with others to encourage them to persevere in the face of adversity. I urge my countrymen to discuss their experiences, or set down their own stories, so that they are not lost forever. They serve as a warning to people of all nations and races to be wary of the danger that can occur when ideology is not subjected to reason. My story is not intended to evoke sympathy or sadness, but to open the reader's mind to what the Cambodian people suffered. Cambodia played host to a million tales of triumph and tragedy, one for each person who lived or died during those terrible years. I hope that the reader will come to the conclusion that even in the darkest of times, hope can endure.

Lim Family Tree

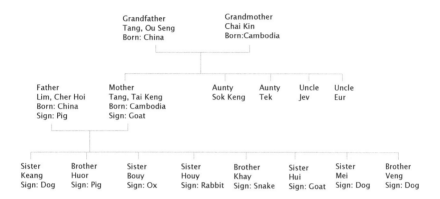

Grandfather
Tang, Ou Seng
Born: China

Grandmother
Chai Kin
Born:Cambodia

Father
Lim, Cher Hoi
Born: China
Sign: Pig

Mother
Tang, Tai Keng
Born: Cambodia
Sign: Goat

Aunty
Sok Keng

Aunty
Tek

Uncle
Jev

Uncle
Eur

Sister
Keang
Sign: Dog

Brother
Huor
Sign: Pig

Sister
Bouy
Sign: Ox

Sister
Houy
Sign: Rabbit

Brother
Khay
Sign: Snake

Sister
Hui
Sign: Goat

Sister
Mei
Sign: Dog

Brother
Veng
Sign: Dog

- I -

Formalities

My father's name was Cher Hoi Lim, and he was born in the Guangdong province of China in 1911. He left behind his wife and son in search of business opportunities and wealth to provide a decent standard of living for his family. Father made his way to *Srok Khmer* (the term Khmer people used to refer to Cambodia) and found that the expanding Vietnam War was making it difficult to travel. He assumed for a while that the region would return to normal, but as time passed it became increasingly plain that he would be unable to return home for some time. Months became years, but events never allowed him to leave. Eventually he accepted the inevitable and began a new life in his adopted country. Though he never spoke of his former life and never returned to his homeland, he continued to send money back to his first wife and son in China until the day he died. Most of his time in Cambodia up until the time he met my mother remains largely a mystery to my entire family.

My maternal grandfather Ou Seng Tang was also initially from China, and also left in search of wealth. He was a bachelor when he arrived in Cambodia and married my locally born grandmother, whose name was Chai Kin. They lived in Kampong Cham, the third largest city in Cambodia, and had two sons and four daughters. One of the daughters died when she was only ten years old, and none of the girls ever went to school. Grandfather held to the belief that it was an unnecessary expense to educate his daughters. It was unseemly, if not actually forbidden, for girls to attend school. He said that he did not want his daughters to be educated; they might write love letters before a suitable marriage could be arranged. One could argue that it was not a very good excuse since many wealthy families sent their daughters to school.

Grandfather supported his family by selling the sort of knick-knacks that can still be bought in Cambodia today for the equivalent of a few dollars. He was on his feet all day carrying a bamboo stick that stretched across his shoulders, with a woven *prakea* basket, containing his livelihood suspended at each end. Grandfather worked hard to put food on the table, mainly rice, which was the staple food and an unofficial second currency in Cambodia. A great deal of maintaining one's status, or '*face*', depended on providing a steady supply of this all too precious commodity. My grandparents were very poor, barely scraping through each day. My grandfather died when his wife was six months pregnant with their youngest son.

My mother's name is Tai Keng Tang. She was seventeen at the time of her father's death, which left the family with no financial support whatsoever. They had no savings and could not rely upon their relatives for support, because Grandfather had died owing them money. Being the eldest child, my mother became the family's provider by making scarves, mosquito nets and robes for the many Buddhist monks in the town. She also sold sweets for cash or in exchange for rice from farmers who had extra grain to trade. After my grandmother had given birth she could again help my mother, along with her two younger sisters, who were fifteen and eleven. The other siblings were too young to be of any help in earning income.

While my mother struggled to keep her family fed, Grandmother was busy entertaining semi-professional matchmakers in order to find a suitable husband for her daughter to marry. Love or personal preference on the part of the bride-to-be was neither here nor there; Grandmother would make the final decision. Matchmakers were usually engaged by the parents of boys, both to speed up the process and to try to ensure a compatible couple. The matchmaker was given a set of criteria and set about finding eligible women, usually beginning with some covert surveillance to find out what the potential brides were like. Once the field was narrowed, neighbours would be questioned about the girl's reputation. Too many boyfriends, a lack of cooking skills, an unkempt house or a history of family disease would halt the process right there. Good looks only came into the equation if specifically requested, and if everything was to the matchmaker's satisfaction, the parents of the girl were then approached.

Grandmother told the matchmakers that her daughter was hard working, frugal with money, a good cook—and just a little feisty. A tendency to speak her mind was not too great a handicap in light of my mother's positive traits, and several proposals were made. Grandmother weighed the various offers as if the nuptials were a potential business deal, trying to ensure that the marriage would help her family get out of its dire financial situation. This was the standard practice at a time when marrying for love was seen as silly, or at least shortsighted. My mother and her husband-to-be never laid eyes on each other before their wedding day.

The time-honoured system of family sponsored courtship failed rather miserably from time to time. Mother divorced her first husband after an unhappy two years in order to escape his drinking, gambling and physically abusive behaviour. They had no children but even so, during that era divorce was a very rare phenomenon in Cambodia, regardless of how badly a husband might treat his wife. Airing one's dirty laundry in public was not at all socially acceptable, and people openly showed their disapproval by gossiping or making snide remarks in order to demean her and the rest of the family. Some people would be nice to her face, and then whisper about her behind her back. Sympathy sometimes had an ugly face. She had to put up with the shame of leaving her husband, and both she and her family were social outcasts until she married my father three years later. It did not matter that she was the one who had been wronged; she was the wife and bore the brunt of blame from relatives and strangers alike. Women were meant to be obedient and unquestioning, which my mother was not when she felt strongly about an issue.

My father had also engaged a matchmaker to find a wife and as before, there was no introduction or consultation with the bride-to-be before the wedding day. Prior to the ceremony, Father's main fear was that he would be presented with a girl with a scarred face. Chinese belief dictated that anyone with deformed features would quite literally be bad for business. This concern was made worse by the fact that mother actively avoided letting any potential suitors see her face. She did not want to be overly forward and sought to appear as a well-behaved girl. Mother had been told that her husband-to-be was wealthy and did not drink or gamble, so a less than perfect face would be just fine by her. Three years after his first Cambodian wife died, Father, who was then forty-five, married my twenty-five year old mother in an elaborate wedding ceremony.

The date for the celebration was chosen by a fortune teller who based her decision on the animal birth signs of the bride and groom. If the lucky day fell at an inconvenient time for those invited, this would not affect the wedding plans at all. People simply had to rearrange their affairs in order to attend. The event was a fusion of traditional Cambodian and Buddhist customs, and the symbol laden ceremonies ran more or less non-stop for three days and nights.

- 2 -

I Do

On the first day of the wedding, events began with prayer at six in the morning, a time at which the air was considered religiously pure. The relatives and friends from the groom's side queued up in pairs, with Father and his best man at the head of each line. Every individual held a tray of food or material offerings, wrapped in fancy paper. The value of the gifts and importance of the guests declined towards the back of the line, with the closest family relatives being at the front. The level of honour that fell on each participant related directly to their position in the procession, and the significance of each was lost on no one. There was no shortage of willing hands at this point in the proceedings because everyone involved was given a gift, usually of money contained in a small red envelope. The more wealthy the family was, the greater the number of gifts and the longer the lines of people to carry them. In the case of my parents, eighteen people proceeded with great fanfare to the front of Mother's house. Eight is a number considered lucky in Chinese; however, eight gifts would be considered too few and eighty-eight impractical. Once they arrived, Father presented Mother's family with the customary gifts of cash and gold, enough to pay for a small house.

Though Father paid for everything, weddings traditionally

took place at the bride's house. Inside, the rooms were already crowded with relatives and guests, with monks chanting prayers and lighting incense sticks that filled the rooms with sweet smelling smoke. More was considered better, to the point where the air was probably hazardous to the health of everyone present. Cambodian women love jewellery, and a wedding provided the perfect occasion to display their wealth. Wrists, necks, ear lobes and any other limbs capable of holding something shiny were festooned with gold and diamonds, each competing with the other in a garish display of prosperity. Subtlety was not a notion to be considered. Despite the unyielding heat of the tropics the ladies' faces were painted with heavy makeup, to the point where they bore little resemblance to their everyday appearance.

Custom made dresses were compulsory for women if they could possibly afford them. They had to be skin tight, no matter the size or shape of the wearer. Looking good was important, but less so than seeming prosperous. It was made sure that other people knew that a dress was new, and recently made for the occasion. A form fitted dress was evidence that it was both recently purchased and not off the rack. Hair was piled high, pinned, coiffed and lacquered to a finish that would survive a minor hurricane.

My mother was wrapped in a glittering gold dress that followed the tradition of Cambodian royalty. Her hair was more sculptured than anyone present and her makeup was as flawless as that seen in any Hollywood production. She was spared the discomfort of high heels as her dress was floor length, making shoes a non-issue. An ornate gold belt held the outfit together, but she wore less jewellery than most of the ladies that were present. There were many gifts of gold chains given to the bride later in the ceremony, so her arms and neck were left bare until then.

My father's wedding attire was neat, clean and irrelevant.

To continue the proceedings, Father and Mother sat on the floor next to each other. They held a traditional pose with bodies leaning forward, elbows cushioned by pillows, legs folded to one side and their palms in prayer position, to face the monks who would bless them. To someone unaccustomed to such contortions it would appear to be an acutely uncomfortable position. It was every bit as painful as it looked, and required both flexibility and stamina to maintain with a smile. The monks took bundles of shredded banana stems and dipped them into a silver bowl of holy water, then sprinkled the liquid blessing over the couple, accompanied by more chanting. A red cotton string was tied onto the right wrists of the new couple, signifying their union as husband and wife. Following that portion of the ceremony, Mother changed into her second outfit of the day. There would be several more to come.

On the second day a tea ceremony was held. Mother presented tea to her parents, and Father presented to a respected elder who acted as a stand-in for his absent family. In return, my parents were given an abundance of gifts. My grandmother gave my mother a gold chain and pendant, and placed it around her neck. A hair cutting ritual followed, which was designed to represent cleanliness and good grooming in the marriage. The bride and groom sat down, and a hired couple sang and danced around them; the woman carrying a mirror and a bottle of perfume, the man with a pair of scissors and comb. They pretended to snip at the newlyweds' hair and sprayed perfume over their heads as a kind of appeal to the Universe. With luck, any spirits that were observing the occasion would be persuaded to keep an eye on the pair, and ensure that husband and wife were always careful to look good to each other.

Some fun was traditionally had at the bride and groom's expense that needed to be endured with good grace. To not participate, or fail to act as if they had not seen it all a dozen times before, would cause a loss of face. There was a huge importance placed on maintaining one's respect in the community, and in order to accomplish this it was sometimes necessary to play the fool. A relative would hold a peeled banana between the couple and ask them to both eat it without using their hands. As the couple leaned forward the relative would pull away the banana, causing the couple's faces to bump into each other. The couple were teased throughout for the amusement of the guests, and presumably the annoyance of the betrothed. — *foreplay as they were strangers*

While the ceremonies were carried out, food preparation went on in the background, making sure that everyone attending was provided with a meal, at any time during the three days and nights. It would be unacceptable for anyone to be the least bit hungry, resulting in much embarrassment. A professional cook was hired and a small army of volunteer women laboured to prepare the huge amounts of ingredients needed. On the final evening they each received a red envelope containing money. No one guest actually attended every ceremony that took place, nor stayed the entire time. People came and went as they pleased and the various events were separated by excessive eating, drinking and gossiping.

On the final night of the wedding, a lengthy and alcohol-fuelled reception was held for three hundred guests. There was no significance to the number; it was merely the total population of the village, minus the people who were working in the kitchen, serving the tables or playing in the band. An eight-course banquet was served, eight being lucky in Chinese culture and just about the number of dishes a guest could comfortably consume.

The guests presented the newlyweds with envelopes of cash upon which were written their names, so that the amount each person gave could later be counted and recorded. This was vital, so that a similar gift could be returned when each of the guests, or their children in turn, were married. Over time a person would attend as many marriages as they themselves had guests at their own wedding, and provided each guest was eventually married then everyone more or less broke even in the end. The whole system might have seemed pointless, but there was indeed a reason. A young couple would receive a large amount of cash with which to begin their married life, and in effect they started out with an interest free loan. Inflation was calculated and gifts were adjusted, according to how much the cost of food rose between one wedding and the next. A person who chose to stay single was out of luck financially because they would still be invited and expected to attend every wedding. In any case, a devoted bachelor or spinster would be an aberration. Marriage was the norm.

On the last night everyone danced to the music of a live band, and the newlyweds worked their way around to each table to thank their guests individually. At midnight and after eighteen hours of celebration, they were the last to leave the reception. Alone for the first time in their lives, the couple finally had the opportunity to actually get to know each other. The exhausting process of becoming husband and wife was over and Mother moved to Kratie where Father ran his business. This is where my parents began their new lives together.

- 3 -

Normality

My Chinese name is Hui and I was born in Kratie (pronounced *kra-cheh*), probably in 1967, as the sixth of eight children. My older siblings in order of birth were sister Keang, brother Huor, sister Bouy, sister Houy and brother Khay. My younger siblings were twins, sister Mei and brother Veng. Mei was the elder by all of twenty minutes, a gulf of time that she never failed to bring up whenever an issue of seniority occurred. Mother was too busy to worry about birthdays, and in fact birthdays were not usually celebrated at all in our family. Only the first month and the sixteenth birthday were recognised, the former to celebrate the baby's survival, and the latter to announce the young adult's eligibility for marriage. She only ever remembered our Chinese animal signs with any degree of certainty, and the true dates didn't really matter.

The Chinese zodiac is a twelve-year cycle of animal signs aligned with twelve different types of personalities. The signs represent how others perceive you and how you present yourself. They are, in order: Rat, Ox, Tiger, Rabbit, Dragon, Snake, Horse, Goat, Monkey, Rooster, Dog and Pig. Since the Chinese zodiac follows the lunar Chinese calendar, the New Year does not begin on 1 January as in the Gregorian calendar, and does not fall on the same date every year. A person who was born in late January or early February may have the sign of the previous year. There is no way of knowing with certainty in which year you were born solely from your Chinese Zodiac sign.

Under this somewhat less than scientific system, all signs have their good points and allow a fortune teller to avoid an unpleasant outcome. It would not be good for business to give a reading that might perhaps affect the client's willingness to pay the fee or to return in the future. Some signs have a rather different interpretation than would occur in other cultures. The sign of the Rat is considered among the best, being ambitious and sincere, generous with financial resources and the leader of the pack. It must have been confusing for the rats who were venerated when in temples, but persecuted with vigour the moment they entered a house. The Ox is also a leader, bright and cheerful. The Tiger possesses great courage and is forthright and sensitive. The Rabbit is a seeker of tranquillity, talented and affectionate. The Dragon is filled with complexity, robust and passionate. The Snake displays great wisdom and is strong willed and intense. The Horse is physically attractive and popular, liking the company of others. The Goat enjoys its privacy, being aesthetic and stylish. The Monkey strives to excel through intelligence and a persuasive nature. The Rooster possesses a pioneering spirit and seeks wisdom and the truth. The Dog is generous, loyal and will work with others. Finally, the Pig is gallant and noble, remaining at your side no matter what.

When I was old enough to comprehend such concepts, Mother told me that I was a Goat. I found this vaguely insulting at the time and did not think I bore much resemblance to the stereotype, but I let the matter drop.

After giving birth to each of her children, my mother underwent a regime to help her recover and restore her strength. This treatment began immediately after delivery, lasted for a month, and would no doubt have horrified most modern doctors. Cambodians believed that the woman's body became cold after giving birth, despite the fact that the temperature in central Cambodia never fell below 25 degrees centigrade. Rather extreme, not to mention uncomfortable, steps were taken to heat up the new mother's body and to prevent further cooling. To aid this, a woman would not take a shower for a month after delivery, although a sponge bath with warm water might be allowed if the birth had been particularly messy. Keeping the body covered from head to toe was important, and often the mother lay on a bed above a fire with her baby in her arms; this was called *ang plueng,* which translates to 'roasting'.

Roasting was believed to prevent illnesses after the birth of a child, a logic I always found rather opaque. New mothers were advised to sit on a rock that had been heated in a fire every morning. It was believed that this prevented the uterus from coming out, presumably on the assumption that nature had not already considered the possibility and taken steps to prevent it. It was also a common practice to place a fire-warmed rock on the abdomen, which was said to make the uterus shrink. It always seemed to me that one practice rather contradicted the other. In any event, the aim was to prevent the sagging of the abdomen after the birth of several children, although many women ended up with scars after falling asleep while clutching a rock left too long in the fire. Steaming the body with boiling water and a mixture of herbs was another post-birth practice designed to make the mother perspire, in the belief that it would remove impurities. After the steaming, some women rubbed pounded turmeric root all over their bodies. It coloured them a golden yellow from head to foot and stained anything they came into contact with. The combination of the steam and turmeric was meant to prevent illnesses and improve the skin.

During the post birth period, women adhered to specific diets which required that they eat very fiery food, usually pork or fish prepared with massive amounts of black pepper or ginger. The food was spicy so that the heat from the food would warm up the body and strengthen the tendons. Women abstained from eating foods such as fruits and vegetables, and this at least was a sensible precaution. Plant based foods were often not cooked enough to remove all bacteria, and fresh salads were usually washed in water that was home to enough life to be visible to the naked eye. Some people recommended that the food be very salty as well as spicy, in order to make the patient thirsty.

A decent thirst was important. It meant that the new mother would consume more of the liquid medicine that was the final part of the post-birth procedure. The remedy was made of herbs boiled in water or rice wine, and taken at every meal. If the rice wine concoction was preferred, a small woman who had almost certainly never before consumed alcohol might find herself moderately drunk for the entire month. This was thought to be a good thing, since an inebriated new mother is likely to sleep, instead of moving about and possibly injuring herself or her child. It was believed that for a period of a month after childbirth, the woman's body was weak and very susceptible to outside forces. She would be cared for by a relative who cooked, cleaned and helped her to look after the baby. The price for not observing these customs was thought to be aches, pains, arthritis and other ailments in later life.

In accordance with Chinese custom, my parents threw an extravagant birthday celebration thirty days after the birth of each and every one of us. Many children did not live to see the end of their first month, and it was considered to be tempting fate to celebrate too soon. The new child was not given a name, and was paid only the barest attention until the time was up. It was believed that evil spirits were less likely to notice the vulnerable newborn if there was no commotion from a premature party or doting relatives. All other birthdays held little meaning compared to that first celebration.

Relatives travelled long distances to attend these events, which in some ways resembled the wedding ceremony that started it all. The new mother was given ample opportunity to show off by changing clothes several times during the course of the event. A live band played at ear-splitting volume and an eight-course meal was served. Red was the predominant colour, money was given in red envelopes and boiled eggs were painted, bright red of course. The relatives and guests presented the baby with gold anklets, bracelets or necklaces. Aside from this, the child played very little part.

For a while I was the youngest child and Father called me *gu niang* (Princess) often enough that I began to believe him. I was less than impressed when the noisy and attention grabbing twins arrived on the scene, although Father still referred to me in royal terms. When the two interlopers were old enough to know the truth, I informed them that I was still the youngest member of the family since Mother and Father were not their parents and that they had, in fact, been found in the rubbish bins outside on the street. This revelation did not seem to bother them in the slightest, and their only comment was a largish spit bubble.

My family lived in a three-storey house newly built by my

father and we were relatively wealthy, having servants who helped to cook and clean. The presence of servants was not as extravagant as it may sound; a live-in maid would work solely for food and a roof over her head, although Father also paid a small allowance.

My father knew of the war over the border in Vietnam and had ordered a cellar built underneath the ground floor for storage, and for just in case of an emergency. I remember it being very dark in the basement, filled with dripping echoes and the scuttling sounds of cockroaches that were big enough to be considered pets. The house was a terrace, tall but very narrow by Western standards, being only four metres wide and fifteen long. This had been the normal house plan ever since a tax had been created years before, which was calculated according to how wide each dwelling was. Pragmatic people that they were, Cambodians immediately responded by changing the shape of their dwellings and a country mansion built by a person who was both wealthy and canny could be an arresting sight. One would find a house completely isolated on all sides, yet it would still be a long and narrow rectangle, three or four storeys high.

Father owned a hardware shop, which he ran out of the ground floor of our house. It was a very practical living arrangement since belongings needed to be constantly guarded against theft. Insurance was unknown and the police were not paid enough to prevent them from supplementing their income in any way they could. Corruption was rife and a small bribe could be relied upon to avoid any official entanglements. Anything you wanted to keep for long had best be kept close by.

The house was at the corner of the Kratie market and overlooked the Mekong River, which lay just to the west. It was an impressive structure for the time, with running water and electricity. Because the water pressure was never very high, the supply only went to the ground floor and the tap ran into a rectangular concrete tub in the bathroom. This arrangement allowed households to store a small supply of water for the frequent periods when the pipes ran dry. Some people kept fish in their tubs and fed them scraps to fatten them up for the table. A shower consisted of repeatedly scooping a small bucket of water out of the tub and pouring it over one's head. We called this bathing method *jung ach*, which is Chinese for 'pour water'. All of the bedrooms were upstairs and the toilet, bathroom and kitchen were on the ground floor near the back door. The front door was a sturdy steel concertina security grill that extended across the entire front of the house's ground level. The river was only a block away from our house and we would walk there to swim and wash our clothes.

Not far from where we lived, we could see rare Irrawaddy dolphins, which made their home in the fast flowing and murky waters that passed by the town. Father said that this was the only place in the whole world where they lived. The dolphins were difficult to spot, since they were seldom prone to the airborne antics of their saltwater cousins. A glimpse of a smooth grey back was the most we could hope for on any given day, although on rare occasions the creatures would rouse themselves to jump clear of the surface if the mood struck them.

My elder sisters Keang, Bouy and Houy did most of the household chores after school and looked after the younger children. I sometimes helped them clean the dishes, hoping for, and sometimes receiving a small allowance from Father. I usually wanted to save the money, but more often than not my youngest sister Mei convinced me to buy sweets instead. She always spent her own allowance on treats for herself, but if her twin brother Veng had any money then she would talk him into buying food and sharing it with her.

Whenever I went to the market with Mei we were terrified of meeting the bogeyman, a character that Mother used to scare us into obedience. She described him in lovingly gruesome detail: a snaggletooth individual, scruffy and dirty, with messy hair. As Mother well knew this was not an altogether uncommon sight in Cambodia. As a result we would stay away from any men that fitted the description whenever we were away from home. The result of being caught by the bogeyman was to be chopped up into little bits and eaten with a sprinkling of fish sauce. Such is the stuff of childhood warnings the world over, although we would later discover that a different form of the bogeyman was indeed on his way. It never entered our nightmares that reality would prove to be far worse than Mother's most dire threats.

During the monsoon season it rained so heavily that it was like a minor waterfall had been called into being directly over our house. We children would run upstairs to the flat concrete rooftop and block the drains with whatever we could find. We played in the pool that formed because of the waist-high brick wall around the outer edge. It was a novelty because most of the water in Cambodia was none too clean, with the Mekong in particular resembling milky coffee. I loved to stand still with my eyes shut, feeling the big clean drops of rain falling on my face. The water would come up to my knees, and we would all run, swim and play in it. I remember enjoying it so much that I would ignore the fact that my knees often scraped painfully on the rough surface. Had we thought about it at all, we might have realised that thousands of litres of water were collecting on the roof in a manner for which it most certainly was not designed. The quality, actually the presence, of reinforcement in the concrete was questionable; building standards were non-existent and if something had given way we could have flooded the house. A sin of that magnitude would have brought hordes of hungry bogeymen to the door to feast on the irresponsible children.

Mother ordered my older brother Khay and I to have an afternoon nap every day, for reasons that were never explained to our satisfaction. We would go up to the first floor and sleep on a big bed that was covered by a mosquito net. The toilet was on the ground floor and we were not allowed to go downstairs during our naptime, so there was a bucket that was placed by the side of the bed. One afternoon we were not in the mood to sleep and decided to instead catch bedbugs, which are tiny flat insects about the size of an apple seed and smelling sweetly of rotten raspberries. The loathsome little things would gather around the corners of the mosquito net, amusing themselves in whatever way bedbugs do while they waited for their next victim. When they sensed a sleeping person they would creep up onto the bed, bite an inconspicuous limb and drink their fill of blood.

We pretended that it was a dark night, so Khay lit a candle and held it in his hand. We crouched on our knees and bent forward to observe the bedbugs closely, without pausing to consider that they might be looking back at us. One of the insects leapt into the air with a tiny click that startled Khay, who promptly dropped the candle and set the mosquito net on fire. I learned that day that there are few things more flammable than fine cotton gauze as flames enveloped the net. We scurried off the bed followed closely by the startled bedbugs, who must have thought that this was a particularly determined attempt to be rid of them once and for all. I stood aside as Khay tried to put out the fire by throwing the half-filled pisspot onto the net, but in his panic he mostly missed. He then started throwing anything he could reach at the conflagration, which only added fuel and caused the flames to rise even higher. We realised that there was no covering this up and that adult help was needed, so we ran downstairs and screamed for help. Our parents came running with buckets of water and the fire was soon out, but everything on and around the bed was burnt, and the ceiling was black with soot.

The anger of my father was a sight to behold. He turned a most alarming shade of red as he strode back and forth shouting about ungrateful, destructive, *wasteful* children that deserved to be locked in the basement with the cockroaches until the bogeyman came to carry them away. We stood trembling as he took his leather belt from his pants and whipped the floor at our feet, loudly promising all the while to make us rue the very day we had been born. But he never laid a finger on us.

I was too young to attend school and did not have a great deal to do at home most of the time. Bug hunting had lost its attraction and there was little chance of my parents providing entertainment. We children were expected to keep ourselves busy and not bother adults unless there was an emergency, such as a minor bedroom fire. Fortunately, the second best thing to school was right next door in the form of a neighbour who made and sold multicoloured rock candy, peanut taffy and candy canes. I loved visiting the neighbour's house and helping to package the candy, after which I was allowed to eat as much as I wanted. Dentists were few and far between, but it was too good an opportunity to pass up.

My elder sister Houy sometimes came with me and helped with the packing process, although she did not quite grasp the work-first-eat-later aspect of the deal. She could never wait to sample the candy but did not want to be caught in the act, so she simply shut her eyes whenever she took a bite. Although Houy would perform this sleight of mouth in full view of the owners, who would comment openly to each other that she was at it again, she never knew they were talking about her. My sister's theory, as she explained it to me later, was that if she could not see them then they would not see her.

One day I had saved some candy for Khay and had just stepped outside to return to our house when an odd tremor ran through the ground. A few seconds later there was a rumbling sound that made me look around for the source, but I could not see anything out of the ordinary. I took a few more steps, but the tremor returned and this time it was a convulsive quake that made me stumble. It was followed by an ear shattering concussion that struck me like an invisible fist. In that single instant everything changed, forever.

- 4 -

On The Menu

The explosions were caused by 1000-pound bombs, dropped by B-52 bombers that flew so high they could not be seen from the ground. On 18 March 1969 the war in Vietnam spilled over the border into Cambodia. More than 3600 B-52 raids were conducted under the codename 'Menu' and over 100,000 tonnes of bombs rained from the sky. The aim of the United States Air Force was the destruction of Vietnamese communist forces in Cambodia in order to prevent them from spreading their ideology. I did not know this at the time; I did not even know what a B-52 was. Answers would have to wait until the world stopped ending for a moment, and I scrambled to the door.

I ran inside and was met by Father, who pushed me into the bomb shelter under our house where the rest of my family was waiting. With only a few candles for light it was very dark and there was water up to our ankles. I was afraid to stand in the water for long because unpleasant creatures often lurked there. Hiding in the dark were rats, cockroaches and giant centipedes that could bite with enough venom to be fatal to a child. There were benches along the walls so I stayed there with my feet drawn up close to my body to stay dry. The cockroaches seemed quite put out that their usual haunt had been commandeered by a pack of humans, and they chittered at us in the dim light. The planes often flew right over Kratie and we could hear the explosions as bombs crashed to earth. We stayed in the shelter for days at a time, for there was no warning before the bombing raids and the first sign of a new campaign would be the obliteration of a patch of countryside the size of a small city. The commotion went on for months, but our house was never hit.

When there was a pause in the bombing raids we would try to maintain some sort of normal life, but the local economy had staggered to a halt. It was almost impossible for goods to be delivered into the town market. Prices rose daily, quadrupled within a week and were ten times normal by the end of the month. The cost of meat and vegetables increased even more rapidly, with the sellers asking for and getting unheard-of prices for common goods. Father refused to buy anything at the new exorbitant rates and believed that the country would return to normal. He emptied the metal safe where he kept all of his money and stuffed as much as he could into a pillow so that he could guard it while he slept.

Mother had a contact in the military, a friend who had heard rumours that had become frequent enough for him to warn her that paper currency could soon plummet in value. She warned Father of these whispers, but he thought the whole notion was silly; after all, every country used money. Mother was convinced though, and spent all of her own savings to buy food for the family. Any money that she did not immediately need was used to buy gold. Father refused to give her any of his cash but she preferred to be cautious, knowing that the precious metal would always be valuable, no matter what happened to the economy.

Eventually, the bombing raids stopped striking the area around Kratie and a restless kind of normality returned to the city. The prices at the market began to fall but never returned to their former level. It seemed as though Father had been right, even if hyper inflation had significantly reduced the value of the paper currency he had gone to such pains to preserve. He returned the cash to its safe during the day, but still removed it to guard at night. Khay began to attend school and I returned to our neighbours to help with their candy operation. Everybody just got on with the business of living as they had before, but something was wrong.

There was an uneasy feeling in the air. It was never anything I could put my finger on, but I felt as though there was a presence that followed me around, pinching me every now and then when I was looking the other way. I was not alone. If any of us children heard an unfamiliar noise or saw anything odd it would send us running for home. It could have just been the natural paranoia anyone would suffer, if aircraft the size of small office buildings had recently dropped high explosives on them. We all felt it, but we had no notion of what was approaching through the jungle from the east. It took three years to arrive.

- 5 -

Year Zero

I was sitting with Mother and telling her about some event of the previous day that was hugely exciting to me, but probably of no great importance. She was listening intently, or at least making a good impression of it, when the kitchen door crashed open. Four young men armed with rifles and dressed all in black barged into our living room and, with absolutely no preamble, yelled at us that we had ten minutes to get out. Mother politely inquired as to what this was all about, but was simply told that we must take our cooking pots and some rice. They would only say that they had orders to evacuate every city and town without exception, and they seemed intent on carrying out those orders to the letter.

Mother was about to protest when the men added that anyone who stayed behind would be punished, and as if to punctuate this threat we heard the sound of a single gunshot from outside. In Cambodia, you learned to obey authority at an early age if you wanted to stay out of trouble or get anything done. Those with power mostly used it for their own gain, and anyone with a sense of self preservation would kowtow to men with guns. The soldiers left as abruptly as they had appeared, but from the sounds of commotion outside, it was plain that they would shortly be back to check on us. Mother immediately retrieved the gold she had been accumulating for some time, and hid it close to her body before she began to gather any other belongings. Father had observed all this in silence, and wrapped his paper money in a bundle of clothes.

My entire family spilled onto the street, along with hundreds of other confused people who were also being driven from their homes. The hundreds became thousands and still no one had any idea of what was happening, where they were meant to go, or why. The soldiers were not interested in explanations, only obedience. I saw hospitals being emptied and the sick carried on stretchers or in the arms of their relatives. People with illnesses or disabilities joined the throng that poured along the main arteries out of the city. Some people were too sick to move under their own power and had no relatives nearby to help. If they did not manage to rouse themselves enough to keep up with the flow, they were roughly pulled out of the crowd. We had our first glimpse of what was to come, as the sick and the old were shot dead and left to rot on the side of the road like garbage.

Kratie was completely evacuated. As we moved out of the town centre we saw that the schools and monasteries were closed, factories were being emptied and the few libraries that existed were burned to the ground. Everyone moved very slowly in the heat of the day, especially thosecarrying large bundles of possessions on their backs. Children cried out in the crowd, becoming separated from their parents, as tens of thousands of evacuees filled the road. Many of them never found their way back to their families and were driven further and further apart by the terrified mass of people. The soldiers sped us up by firing their weapons over the heads of the crowd, or at the feet of individuals who did not move quickly enough for their liking. The gunfire only increased the chaos and panic, and I saw people literally walked to death as the pace of the forced march took its toll. They collapsed by the side of the road and either stayed where they lay, or forced themselves to their feet to totter on a bit further. Those who fell were lost from view as the crowd moved on, and I heard an occasional gunshot delivered by one of the more zealous soldiers—or more merciful.

My family had been lucky in that we were at least allowed a few minutes to gather some belongings, but we had to leave behind anything that we could not carry. We took no official papers or family photos. There was no arguing with the soldiers and any dissent was met by immediate punishment, which we were told was for our own good. Kratie was left as a virtual ghost town and although we did not know it at the time, the same scene was being played out across Cambodia. The wave of soldiers swept across the country from east to west, and almost every person was driven into the jungle at the point of a gun.

Although I called them *yothea* ('soldiers'), they were in reality mostly twelve and thirteen-year-old boys who wore black clothing and sandals made from old car tyres. The only colour about them was their red *kroma* scarves that each wore wrapped around his head or neck. They were illiterate peasant youths that had been recruited from the poorest villages, given some rudimentary training and armed with assault rifles. The soldiers called themselves the 'Khmer Rouge', and they were proud to be in this new army. They felt that they had gained honour by being the ones the new regime could trust. History itself was declared dead, and 'year zero' thus began. The soldiers sang what was to be Cambodia's national anthem and told us about the new government: *Angkar*. We were to be guided by a gentle leadership that would usher in a glorious new age, one where all would be equal and all would work for the common good. A country that would have no use for the corrupting influences of other societies, one that would be built on the hard work of the people, for the good of the people.

The child soldiers of *Angkar* acted as people usually do when they are suddenly granted authority where previously they had none. They abused it. They fired their weapons into the air to force us along and savagely beat anyone who did not immediately obey. We were told that the Americans were on their way to bomb the city, which was a lie, but like all the best lies it possessed a certain credibility. The fact of the matter was that the United States had indeed seemed intent on bombing everything and everyone in Cambodia for quite some time. In the absence of a reliable news source people tended to believe almost anything they were told, and so we ran, walked and finally staggered into the jungle. We had few food supplies or clothes, and I walked at first through the streets and then across the fields, until blisters rose and burst on my feet. What little I had packed was carried in a bundle on my shoulder, and although it was not much I had to carry it for many miles over rough ground. I kept telling myself that this was just a temporary thing, that soon we would all go back to our house and things would return to normal.

The soldiers forced us to march for six hours to a town in the middle of the jungle, far away from our house and from every-thing we knew. I do not know exactly where we were taken, but we were told that this *phum* village was to be our new home. The scene that greeted us was quaint, picturesque, and everything that a tourist might imagine when they think of a secluded jungle retreat. Looks aside, it was primitive and dirty, and we would have given anything to return to our house in Kratie. But at least we were together.

We were allocated a hut that was built on stilts, with a bamboo ladder leading up to the front door and a thatched roof of layered palm leaves. The inside of the shack comprised a single room for ten people, with no beds or furniture. We ate and slept on a bare bamboo floor, and had no electricity or running water. Security was minimal at best, so Father jammed a beam of wood across the door from the inside to act as a crude lock. The kitchen was on the ground under the house and our stove was made up of three equally sized rocks arranged in a triangle, so that a pot could be balanced on top. We stored water in two big clay pots on the ground by the side of the house. They had to be filled by fetching the water a bucket at a time, from a hand-pumped well some distance away. This water was for cooking and drinking only, and we had to clean the pots regularly to reduce the build-up of slime. The pots had to be covered to prevent malaria-carrying mosquitoes from breeding in the still water.

When I had left Kratie I had been wearing my favourite sandals, which strapped around my ankles and were rather fashionable, in my opinion. It was hard to imagine footwear that was less appropriate for a jungle hike, although at the age of six I was unacquainted with high heels. My sandals had taken quite a beating on the journey from the village, and quickly fell apart in the dirt, heat and damp of our new home. I would have soon outgrown them in any event, and I wanted a pair of sandals fashioned out of car tyres, like the soldiers wore. They were ugly but also practical, and the only option available.

We quickly ran out of toothpaste and brushes. I brushed my teeth with my finger wrapped in a small piece of cloth and dipped into a mixture of powdered charcoal and salt, or wood ash. It was not particularly effective or pleasant tasting, but there was no alternative and it seemed better than nothing. Soap and shampoo were also rapidly depleted so everybody smelt the same, which is to say, badly, but we ceased to notice. Our toilets, such as they were, were fifty metres away and simply a hole in the ground with two planks of wood on either side to squat on. Sitting as one does on a Western toilet was out of the question, but that was no problem since squatting was the usual method anyway. It also had the advantage of allowing for a quick getaway from a smell that defied description. I would clamp my nostrils shut with thumb and forefinger every time I had to use the toilet. Even though I spent as little time there as possible, I could not help but notice the writhing mass of maggots in the pit below. A spade-full of dirt replaced a flush and itchy leaves served as toilet paper.

There was no money in circulation, and no markets to buy or sell goods if there had been. Newspapers, private property, schools and holidays had all been abolished. Family life and freedom of movement was restricted and religious practices were completely forbidden. Any sort of motorised transport became increasingly uncommon and people walked everywhere they went, not that there was anywhere to go. It took a long time, but Father finally realised that his money was no longer of any use. The notes were now worthless, and to be found harbouring currency was to put you and your family in great danger. Father was nothing if not stubborn though, and still could not bring himself to destroy the evidence of his former life as a businessman. My eldest sister Keang was afraid of what would happen to us all if the Khmer Rouge ever found the bundle of money, so one day she ran home ahead of everyone else and burned the lot to ashes. Father was angry at first, but he quickly calmed down and I think that he was actually relieved to be rid of the incriminating notes.

The networks of family relationships and contacts that we had built in Kratie were broken and gone. We found ourselves in a place where we did not know anyone we could trust. It was not that the people we lived among were particularly unworthy of our faith, just that we could not take any chances in the light of recent history. We were fearful and disoriented in our new surroundings, which seemed to be exactly the desired effect. Under those circumstances, no organised opposition to the new regime could develop. If one was feeling particularly charitable, they could believe that the motivation for the evacuation was *Angkar*'s ideological commitment to the creation of a one-class state. Either way, the purge of the cities was designed to remould the Cambodian population into a compliant workforce.

The Khmer Rouge believed that manual work would transform us from budding capitalists into simple labourers on agricultural communes. They would overcome with a single stroke every distinction of class and status. City dwellers were considered evil and corrupt, parasitically drawing their sustenance from the countryside like a leech on the body of the nation. We were seen as conduits for the influence of foreign lands, particularly America. Purification of those contaminated by city life could apparently only come through physical contact with the land itself. Now that we were trapped we were told at great length of the plans of our new leaders. I did not know why they bothered. The words made no sense to me, but they were the ones with the means of persuasion and a bullet beats logic any day of the week. We were expected to be masters of our environment, virtually self-sufficient in providing our own food and as many basic needs as possible. We knew nothing of the events occurring in the outside world. For us, the rest of the planet had effectively ceased to exist.

Angkar ordered us to rid ourselves of anything that could be traced back to the American imperialists. It was a rather vague demand, which turned out to mean such things as watches, necklaces, bracelets, diamond rings, gold bullion and anything else of real value. These things were declared impure and we were forbidden from possessing them. In reality, separating people from their gold takes rather more than mere threats to their life. My parents handed in just enough to allay the soldiers' suspicions, and hid the rest. After this process had run its course, the Khmer Rouge faithful openly sported a surprising amount of confiscated jewellery. It was odd, given that they were meant to be the most pure of the new order, but presumably they were immune to its corrupting influence.

We were easy targets because despite having been born in Cambodia, none of us children spoke the Khmer language beyond the very basics. Father did not hold the native population in high regard, and he had insisted that we speak only Chinese at home. Uttering any language but Khmer was an invitation to a beating or worse, so we had to stutter and mumble as if we were simpletons. The local villagers teased us mercilessly, although it was quite some time before we gained enough fluency to realise what they had been saying. We had to learn fast.

There were a few trees around our hut: mango, tamarind and guava trees that were heavy with fruit. We grew sweet potato vines, which are fast growing, ground covering plants. We had the choice of eating their young shoots as they grew, or waiting until the tubers formed under the ground. The potatoes grew best in sandy soils with lots of sun and space. The hotter the temperature the faster they grew, which was fortunate, because heat was one commodity that Cambodia had in abundance. Wet ground produced small, bent and forked potatoes that were hard to peel, so we built rows of raised beds to improve the drainage. A hibiscus tree grew near the front door which blossomed with red flowers that had sweet nectar inside, and I ate them as a poor substitute for the candy I used to get from our neighbours. I wondered often where they were, and if they still made their treats.

At this time we had just about enough rice and vegetables to live on, but protein was in very short supply and we had to learn to be resourceful. We would find and catch anything that moved, including wild tarantulas that are a traditional delicacy in Cambodia, although a hairy one. During mating season the male tarantulas left their burrows to seek willing females, and they could then be found wandering around. Rain also forced them out of their holes in search of higher ground, or if they were reluctant to emerge we would poke a long stick into their burrows. If all else failed we lit a fire and smoked them out, which would send the spiders running out of the silk flaps that covered their escape routes. They were big and intimidating, but also harmless and capable of no more than a minor nip. We had far more to fear from an average mosquito. The tarantulas were cooked in a fire to burn off all their hair; I preferred the females, because they had larger abdomens with creamy soft centres surrounded by the crunchy legs.

We also caught cockroaches, which were believed to cure the hacking coughs that people would often suffer in the unsanitary conditions. We caught the large black insects by simply grabbing them with our hands, but occasionally we were too aggressive and crushed them in our palms. Squashed Cambodian cockroach smelled like cola soda to me, and forever afterward whenever I encountered cola I was reminded of cockroach juice. The roaches were destined to be crushed anyway, mixed with water and the concoction drunk as a hideously unpleasant medicine. It probably did no good, but it certainly made us stifle our coughs to avoid the cure.

Rhino horn was another substance used for medicinal purposes. Believed to cure fever in traditional Chinese medicine, it was frequently used to treat life-threatening illnesses. The horns are made of keratin and are the same stuff that makes up human hair and fingernails, but in the absence of anything better we ground the rhino horn on a granite dish, adding water to assist with the process. It would become a powdery mixture that tasted like chalky water, which we drank when we were ill. Its effectiveness, such as it was, seemed to closely match the strength of the patient's belief in its healing properties.

Another source of food was 'apple' snails, which we would hand pick from ponds, rice fields and trenches. The name of the snails was a clue as to their size, and one of them would cover the palm of my hand. Most animals in Cambodia gave humans a wide berth in case they ended up in the pot; the snails did their best, but they were not the swiftest of creatures. To prepare the snails, we first had to remove the shell door and then dig the body out with a long thorn or stick. As a defence against predators the internal organs tasted awful, so we would remove the intestines of the snail by pulling away the main body, leaving behind the more palatable foot.

One day my father became very ill, and that same night an owl flew into one of our mango trees, hooting non-stop for hours. Mother said that this type of bird only came to the house when people inside were near death. The owl was thought to be evil, and many people in Cambodia believed that when an owl cries it is about to take someone's life, and that their spirit would fly away with the bird. When we heard the owl that night we thought that it might be my father's time to die. I remember Mother cursing loudly at the owl and finally she told us to drive it away. We started to shout at the bird, but it just watched our antics with its huge eyes and seemed to be more entertained than afraid. It was only encouraged to leave when we started throwing burning sticks into the tree, and we felt that our efforts had been rewarded when Father got better soon afterwards.

On arrival we had been granted a small plot of farm land, but we needed help to plough the ground. Mother bought a female cow from one of the local villagers in exchange for some of her hidden gold. She was hoping to profit by eventually getting the animal to produce a calf that she could sell or trade. In the meantime we used the cow to plough the field so that we could plant sweet potatoes. Guiding a primitive plough behind the cow was backbreaking work, but much preferred to digging the ground by hand. As it turned out the cow did get pregnant and gave birth, but she became extremely protective of the calf in the process. She would charge at anyone who came near the calf, which made almost everyone afraid to go near her.

All of us children were together one day when the cow took exception to our presence and charged towards us. She was taller at the shoulder than me and bigger than all of us combined, so naturally we scattered. I did not stop until I reached the safety of a tree, and when I finally looked back I saw that Khay had returned to our hut and found an axe. He was now standing his ground as four hundred kilograms of enraged bovine raced towards him with lowered horns. At the last second Khay stepped neatly aside and swung his weapon overhand, cracking the cow squarely between the eyes with the blunt side of the axe head. She stopped dead in her tracks, plainly stunned by this turn of events, and looked Khay up and down. She backed off, shaking her head as if to clear it, then charged again and received another blow to the skull for her trouble. She got the message after a while that Khay was not someone to trifle with and that he would never, ever back down. From that time on he was the only one of our family who could control her, and so he would take her to plough the fields.

There were no cars or any form of motorised transportation in the village where we lived at that time. Ox carts were used for heavy hauling and there were not even any bicycles. On rare occasions we would see a truck passing the bamboo huts, raising a miniature dust storm in its wake as it drove along the dirt road that ran through the village. This would always be the cause of great excitement among the children. We saw very few examples of technology and the huge noisy machines were fascinating, or at least different, to the usual scene of rice fields and cows. We would chase after the trucks on foot, counting the number of wheels they had until we were exhausted from trying to keep up. We loved the smell of the exhaust and would inhale deeply so that the fumes filled our lungs. It was not exactly clean country air, but we found our fun where we could.

At first my family were all together in the village, crowded into a hut the size of our living room back in Kratie. Things began to change though, as *Angkar* tightened its grip on Cambodia and continued to spread their rule. After about six months an order was announced: all of the older and able-bodied people were to travel to farms far away to help with the rice harvest. One day they were there and the next they were gone, leaving my sister Houy to care for me, Mei and Veng. Houy was eleven, I was seven and the twins were four—or four plus twenty minutes, Mei insisted. Houy organised for us all to work together so that we could scrape together enough food to live. The rations we received from the Khmer Rouge were measured in accordance with how many family members there were, and how much work each of them could perform. Four young children could do very little and we received only a tiny amount of food. What we were given or found just had to do until our parents returned. They were gone for three months at a time, and the hot weather of the tropics meant that there were three harvests per year, so they could not stay for long when they did visit.

The Khmer Rouge doled out portions of unhusked rice by measuring it into woven baskets, each differently sized depending on who was receiving the grain. Adults got larger rations, and the basket used for children was depressingly small. There was no accounting for the fact that growing children might actually need more food; the work we could perform was all that mattered to *Angkar*. It was up to us to make our rice last until the next distribution, an exercise in self-control to which we younger children were ill suited. In this regard though, Houy ruled us with an iron fist and right from the start she made sure that we ate only the minimum. We never completely ran out.

We had to process our own rice using a traditional method that for a child was at first fun, but soon wore thin. The first stage in milling was to remove the husk, and the brown grain that resulted still contained the germ and outer bran layers. We then had to remove those to expose the white starch centre, which was polished to produce white rice. The golden paddy rice was placed into a traditional milling machine, which consisted of a solid fixed circular base and topped with a matching cylinder, both of which were made of fired clay. The top was rotated by means of an arm that was pushed and pulled by one or two people.

The rice was poured into an opening in the top and made its way through to the gap between the two cylinders. Here it was ground between the hard clay surfaces to remove the husk. The rice and husks fell from the sides of the contraption, leaving the grain ready for polishing. An adult would operate the machine by simply standing in one place and pushing the bar back and forth, but the twins and I were too short. We had to hang on to the bar, which was over our heads, and run back and forth as Houy fed rice into the top cylinder. Because of her height, and our lack of it, she ended up doing most of the work herself. The milling machine was owned by one of our neighbours and its use had to be paid for with some of the finished rice.

We placed the de-husked rice into a large wooden mortar buried in the ground. Above the mortar was a vertical pole to act as the pestle, connected to a horizontal arm like a seesaw. The operator would step on the end of the arm to raise the heavy pestle, and then release it to drop onto the rice. An adult could do this single handed, but we were so small that it took two of us at once. The action of the pestle smashing into the grain removed the final bran layer, which then had to be separated from the white rice. To accomplish this we poured a couple of kilograms of grain at a time into a flat bamboo basket, and then repeatedly flicked the rice into the air and caught it, which allowed the lighter material to blow away. Finally, any rice that still had some husk attached was removed by tilting the basket and moving it in a circular motion, much like panning for gold. The finished rice would end up at the high side of the basket, and the portion with husks still attached collected at the bottom. The unfinished rice then went back into the mortar and the process was repeated until only white rice remained.

The husks, bran and tiny pieces of broken rice were not discarded; in fact nothing was ever wasted. We mixed the husks with chopped up banana trees to feed to a pig that Mother had acquired from a local villager. Their distrust of the new arrivals from the city had been overcome by a small amount of gold, and the deal had to be struck in absolute secrecy in case the Khmer Rouge found out. We had to walk a long way to find the banana trees because there *were* none in the rice paddies that surrounded the village. A banana tree was easy to cut down, but they contained a lot of water and were very heavy to carry back home on our shoulders. At the time, everything seemed far away and heavy.

Khay was nine years old when he came back to visit us from a distant farm where he was living with Mother, Father, Keang, Huor and Bouy. He had soon had enough of our dreary new life, and drew Mei and Veng and I into a game of hide and seek in the rice fields. It was a rare occasion for us to have any fun at all, and we were determined to make the most of the opportunity to just act like kids again. After about thirty minutes the game was abruptly called to a halt when Mei tripped over in the rice stalks and fell, dislocating her right elbow in the process. Her arm dangled uselessly as she cried in pain.

Khay ripped the offending rice stalks from the ground and used them to wrap her elbow, all the while chanting random words of healing. He did this in imitation of the monks who used to be a common sight throughout Cambodia, but who were by now de-frocked or murdered. His reasoning was that if the rice stalk had hurt her elbow then using it as a bandage should reverse the damage, via some sort of sympathetic magic. No one else had a better idea, but it did not work and Mei's elbow began to swell alarmingly, so we all went back to the hut where Houy was waiting. At eleven she was the oldest member of our family within miles, but she deferred back to Khay, who always bossed around any child under the age of fifteen. He usually sorted things out for himself, but he knew when it was time to get some adult help.

The next day, Khay walked with Mei all the way back to the rice farm where he had left our parents the day before. They could not spare her too much time—under the watchful eyes of the Khmer Rouge everyone had to spend all day working in the fields. Mei was left alone in the hut while everyone else was away, with nothing to occupy her but to eat some cooked rice. Each morning a large snake would come into the hut and climb up to the beam that held the roof aloft. It was probably only seeking shelter during the hottest part of the day, but to Mei's young eyes Death himself had come to call. The snake was plainly waiting to catch her off guard and swallow her whole. To add insult to potential injury, the snake departed every afternoon before the others returned, and no one believed that it was ever there.

Each morning before Mother left for work in the fields, she sprayed spit over the protesting Mei's injured arm and then yanked hard on it. This caused enough pain for the four-year-old to swear imaginatively each and every time. Mother did not have any experience in the matter; she was just trying to force the arm back to where it was meant to be. After a week of this regime, Mei's limb was yanked back into its proper place with a muffled click. There were no longer any doctors to care for an injured child, and her own mother had been forced to leave her alone all day. If it was not for Mother's intuition and desperate treatment, Mei's arm would have quickly become useless and she would have been crippled for life. The spitting had probably not helped, but one never knew.

In the monsoon season everything was wet or at least damp, for weeks at a time. I acquired a fungal skin infection between my toes and the skin became cracked, sore and itchy. Shoes were a distant memory and I never did manage to get a pair of the robust sandals worn by the soldiers, so I walked everywhere on my unprotected feet. I did not know it at the time, but my affliction was of the same kind that had afflicted tens of thousands of US soldiers across the border in Vietnam. I was told that the cure was to put my infected foot into a pot filled with urine, which I had to supply, every day for a week. Either the fungus or the pee made my skin start to peel away from my toes, leaving it red raw. To help with the itchiness I tried to keep my foot dry and warm, but the monsoon made that impossible. Eventually the rains ended and the fungus went away on its own.

We ate what we could grow, catch or pick in the jungle, with the majority of our protein coming from insects, birds, and on very rare occasions, our own animals. We owned a few chickens, a pig, a cow and a calf, but we were lucky to have meat once a month. When we did, it was usually from some wild animal that had not been quick enough on its feet. Mother bartered the cow and calf in exchange for two female buffalo, which were stronger and better able to haul the plough through the fields. There were no medicines for the people, let alone for livestock, and when our animals became ill there were no vets to treat them. If an animal seemed certain to die then we would kill it and make the most out of the situation. One day our pig fell sick and seemed to be on a rapid slide to death. Before it could lose too much weight, Father killed it by making a small incision in the neck and cutting its wind pipe. I was upset because I had been fattening the pig by feeding it for quite a while, and even though it was not a pet it had been a personable and friendly animal, as pigs usually are. For a seven-year-old child with no possessions and little else to do apart from work, the animal had been a welcome distraction.

At that time there were no pets in Cambodia. Everything that was alive, not immediately useful, and not actually human, was viewed as a potential meal. We drained the blood from the pig by holding it upside down and collecting the rich red fluid in a bowl. After adding some salted water and stirring, the blood congealed into blood jelly or 'blood tofu'. The result looked like a square slab of liver that was cut into rectangular pieces, rinsed in water and cooked. The jelly was eaten in soups or put into rice porridge.

After the pig had been drained of blood, we placed it whole onto a fire to burn off its hair, and then used a knife to scrape away any scorched bristles that remained. Even if we had not been short on food there would have been nothing wasted, and absolutely every part of the animal was used. Aside from the meat and fat we ate the offal, which included the liver, heart, lungs, tongue, ears, brain, eyes, nose and stomach. Bones became soup and the marrow extracted, cartilage was eaten with relish and the leftovers from a sizable pig amounted to nothing more than a small pile of bones. In Southeast Asia many organs and animal parts are used for food or traditional Chinese medicine. Pork was the most common meat, so popular pork dishes include stir-fried kidneys, intestine slices and the ever-present blood jelly. Some of the odd parts of the animal, commonly discarded in other cultures or used for pet food, were the most highly prized. There was a lot of meat on a pig but there were only ever small amounts of eyes, ears and brains. Eating the brain was believed to increase intelligence, and even reproductive organs had their own recipes. Pig uterus stewed with ginger might have been an acquired taste, but then so were many other dishes that people ate when there was no room for waste.

When it was time to prepare our chickens for eating, we would catch them by the legs and pluck the feathers around their necks. Needless to say the chickens vigorously objected to this, and had to be tightly held to prevent their escape. We would slit their throats and cut the wind pipe, then hang them upside down and collect the blood in a bowl, much in the same way as we had with the pig. The chickens were let go to run around headless until the nerves stopped firing and they dropped to the ground. Finally, a dip in boiling water made the feathers easy to pluck. Obviously animal welfare was not high on the list of priorities in this process, but it was designed to provide the maximum amount of food. The comfort of the unfortunate bird became a minor consideration when one had been eating cockroaches for a while.

My older brother Khay was always trying to improve our situation. Whenever he returned from the rice farms, he would draft me to help carry out a seemingly endless series of schemes. I think this was partly because I could follow instructions, and partly because I was small. My size was handy in certain situations that required a degree of infiltration. He was two years older and age equated to wisdom, so it never occurred to me to question his plans. He was completely fearless and had an answer for everything—often a wrong answer, but he was rarely afflicted by doubt. He would pluck a plan out of thin air and follow it through with a determination that regularly got us both into trouble. He was a born leader if ever there was one.

Khay never allowed anyone to pick on his brothers and sisters, especially the younger ones. One day I was playing with the neighbour's children and one of them hit me for some reason or other. I went home and told Khay, who immediately went to exact revenge on my behalf. I do not know precisely what happened next, but the other child never laid a hand on me again. Khay would order us about in the expectation that we would obey him, and we did. It was a mystery where he had come by such an air of command, but there was no doubting that he had it. Many of my family would eventually owe their lives to Khay. He was my mentor, my protector and my hero.

Poultry of any sort was a rare treat, and so Khay invented a contraption for trapping birds. It was an arrangement of sticky tar on a piece of wood, with some bait at its centre. When the bird landed to eat, it would become stuck on the tar and Khay or I would race to catch it before it could extricate itself. There was no such thing as a protected or inedible species in those days and any catch was proudly carried home. Compared with cockroach juice, roasted sparrow was very fine fare indeed.

Sweets were a thing of the past, but there was sugar to be had if one was game and knew where to look. Khay, Mei, Veng and I decided to raid a nearby beehive that was hidden by the jungle. The hive was in a tree and out of our reach, so Khay started to hurl rocks at it in an attempt to knock it down. The bees were having none of this, and swarmed out to defend their home. We started to run away but Khay told us to crouch down, pretend to be rocks and the bees would ignore us. We followed his instructions, but the bees immediately saw through our disguise and continued to press their attack. Jumping into the pond never occurred to us, and when we could take the stings no longer we ran for home, with a cloud of enraged insects following us all the way. Once inside I started to pull the bees off my body, but that just left the stings behind with their venom sacks attached and still pumping poison into my skin. I was stung so badly that I was ill for days afterwards. We gained no honey that day, but we did learn a healthy respect for the intelligence of the bees.

We took great pains in attending to our water buffaloes, and took them to bathe at a nearby pond at the end of each day. In order to keep the buffaloes under control they had a ring through their sensitive nostrils, to which we would tie a rope and lead them. We could tie the end of the rope to a tree and leave them to graze, returning a couple of hours later to move them to a new area. In the meantime, we would search for something for lunch and some clean water. As we started to head for home one evening, I saw a massive *chleung* leech as thick as my wrist firmly clamped onto one of our buffalo's flanks. I had always been afraid of leeches and I was too terrified of the ugly thing to try to remove it myself, so I let it drop off on its own after it had drunk its fill of blood.

Young though we were, we never carried any food with us when we took the buffaloes out to graze. We would eat whatever we could find, such as flowers, rose apples, roots, insects and wild grapes. The grapes made my throat itchy, and Khay told us that if we barked like a dog after eating each grape it would stop the irritation. I tried this but it did not work at all. There were few alternatives that day though, so I continued eating the grapes and drank a lot of water afterwards. We also had to find vegetables, fruit and fish to take home for dinner. We caught fish by building a mud dam across a pond and then draining one side. This process was as laborious as it sounds, and meant using a basket woven from local vegetation as a bucket, or sometimes just by cupping our hands to splash the water from one side of the makeshift dam to the other. It took hours to drain the water to the point where we were knee deep in the mud and could see the fish. We carried the fish home on our shoulders by hooking a vine through their gills.

In the dry season most of the ponds dried up, leaving behind mud that cracked under the hot sun. Eels, frogs and crabs waited out the lack of water by hiding underneath the surface, where it was still wet and cool. We caught the eels by lifting up the cracked mud and turning it over with our hands. The eels were so fast and slippery that we had to resort to using our teeth in order to keep hold of them.

All of this foraging in and around the ponds near the village led to me getting a nasty roundworm infection. Parasitic round-worms can live on or in humans and they can cause a variety of health problems. The eggs lay in the soil and enter the body when a person inadvertently touches them and then transfers them to the mouth. They can also enter the body directly through the skin, finally ending up in the intestines as adults. Mature roundworms feed by attaching themselves to the walls of the gut and leeching blood, which is stripped of its nutrition. The worms affected millions and contributed to malnutrition and anaemia in people who could not afford it.

The worms caused my stomach to swell out like I was a skinny and pregnant seven-year-old child, as opposed to merely a skinny one. I always felt hungry and had an itchy bottom, but when I went to the toilet I found that only worms came out. Khay told me to eat the foliage of tamarind and guava trees, because the tamarind leaves were sour and the guava leaves were bitter. The theory was that the worms would not like the combination any better than I did, and would either die or be persuaded to depart on their own. It seemed like a reasonable idea as these things went, and certainly worth a try, but I ended up playing host to the worms for quite a long time, as did most of the children in the village.

Even before the rule of the Khmer Rouge the notion of family was porous in Cambodia. Families with plenty of children might give one or more away to people who had few or no offspring of their own. This was not merely a matter of convenience and was usually done to provide a better life for the child.

Before I was born, Mother had promised my aunt Sok Keng that she could have her next girl. My aunt had two sons and no daughter, so I suppose this was to balance things out. Before the Khmer Rouge came I had been sent to live with her, my uncle and their sons. My aunt was less well off than my family, and had lived in the country with animals running around everywhere. There was barely a paved road to be seen and after half a day I declared that a princess should not have to stay in such a place. I had returned to my family that evening.

Things were different now that the Khmer Rouge was in charge. With the new circumstances of our family and after no discussion with me, Mother gave me away to a Cambodian family that had only one son. The family owned a custard apple farm and I would undoubtedly have been better off in a material sense. The couple came to visit us just once, and when they were ready to return home I was told—to my great horror—that I would also be leaving to live with them. Mother told me that they had plenty of food and that I would never go hungry again.

My youngest sister Mei was also given away to another family at the same time. Her situation was similar to mine in that the family had only one son, and she too would be cared for and well fed. Although she was only four years old, she was not about to take the move lying down. She could not understand anything the family was saying and cried so much that the adoptive family had no choice but to return her to my parents. She was back by the end of the day.

I was slightly older and a very obedient child, so I did as I was told. I asked no questions, even though I had no idea of why I was leaving or for how long. The family was very good to me and let me eat as many custard apples as I liked. Their son tried to befriend me, but I was scared of him because he was so tall and had very dark skin, with stark white teeth when he smiled. I do not remember how long I stayed with the family, but I do remember that even though I was treated kindly and was always well fed, I felt miserable. I missed my brothers and sisters and would lie in bed every night until I quietly cried myself to sleep. I felt utterly alone and would rather have lived with my family with too little to eat, than with strangers who had plenty of food. After some time it became obvious to the couple that I was miserable, and they sent me back to my family. I was elated to return, running to my brothers and sisters and hugging them all. Mother commented to Father that it was much easier to give away a child before they could talk back.

In many parts of Asia, having white skin was considered to be a mark of beauty and was very desirable. This prompted the sale of many creams and potions that were claimed to reverse the effects of the sun. The fashion had a practical if banal use; it marked those of fair skin as not being field workers, out in the blazing sun each day. People wore wide hats and long sleeves to ward off the effects of the sun when they had to be outdoors. Men who were used to giving orders grew the nails on their little fingers as long as they could. They obviously did not do hard work if they were able to maintain their nails in perfect condition, and it was a status symbol to do so. People with dark skin and rough hands were looked down upon as manual labourers. Worse, they were thought to be descended from the original indigenous population, who were considered to be of a lower class and beyond the help of education. The elite never paused to consider that others might have been just as capable as themselves, if they were just given an opportunity.

This none too subtle discrimination took a nasty turn for the pampered city people—or so the new regime saw my family—when we were forced into the countryside. Suddenly, having pale skin marked us out as being the capitalists who had caused the misfortunes of the Cambodian people for so long. The traditionally uneducated country folk were put in charge overnight, and were hailed as the pure citizens of the new order. Many of these people remained uninterested in power games; they simply wanted to get on with the business of life and to treat all people equally and with respect. Others took great delight in the reversal of their fortunes. They wanted retribution for the real or imagined injustices of the past, and took revenge on families who were allegedly part of the corrupt capitalist class. In a repetition of other places and times the Khmer Rouge found plenty of excuses for their atrocities. It was standard practice for brutal regimes to provide their supporters with a focal point for their discontent. *Angkar* needed someone to hate.

We were it.

- 6 -

In Plain Sight

We lived for two years in that small village, left to fend for ourselves in complete poverty although in relative peace compared to the upheaval that had taken us there. But it was not destined to last, and in 1975 we were ordered to move to a new village deeper in the heart of Kratie *Khet* province. We were only given a few hours notice of the shift, but we had very little to pack. I still did not understand what was going on or why, but when my parents told us that we must move, we went without complaint. The relocations were possibly part of *Angkar's* master plan, or just to keep the population off balance and under control. We carried what food we had and walked for days through the jungle, barefoot in most cases. The wilds of Cambodia are not places to travel without footwear, and we all accumulated an impressive collection of blisters, cuts and infections.

Our carefully tended and precious buffaloes were confiscated and we never saw them again. Mother did not protest; she understood that it would have done no good and might have landed her and her family in serious—possibly fatal—trouble. After all, she had bought the cow that was later traded for the buffaloes with gold that she had sworn she did not possess. The Khmer Rouge were prone to punishing people for little or no reason, and a lie about hidden gold would have been certain to bring down their wrath, if for no other reason than there might be more to steal. Whether any of my family was guilty of anything or not, the relocation marked the beginning of our descent into a hellish existence that we would be lucky to emerge from alive, let alone unharmed.

In the new village half the people were *pracheachon chas,* the original inhabitants who had lived in the area for generations. The other half were *pracheachon tmey,* new people like us who had been marched in from the city. The jungle villages typically comprised about two hundred families, each housed in a one-room hut four metres on each side, which was about a quarter of the size of our previous dwelling. The huts were constructed on stilts and protected from the elements by a thatch of woven dried leaves, more or less identical to the village we had just left. They were also suspiciously new, which meant that someone, somewhere, had been planning the whole move for some time. It all seemed very similar to where we had come from in that there was no furniture, electricity, running water or toilets. I quickly realised that there was one major difference though. There were no kitchen areas underneath the huts and in fact, there did not seem to be any cooking facilities at all. Less visible were the policies of our new existence. My three oldest siblings Keang, Huor and Bouy were immediately sent away to join the youth brigades called *kong chalet.* The rest of us were apparently not yet old enough to be of any use in the labour camps, so we remained in the village with our parents. At least I still had Khay with me for a while.

One mystery was solved when we found out that cooking in the huts was outlawed, and that it had been decreed that everyone in the village would eat together in a common area. The Khmer Rouge demanded that all families turn in their kitchenware as well as their food supplies, and nobody was permitted to eat outside of the dining hall. The food consisted of *congee*, a rice porridge that can be a tasty and substantial meal when meat, eggs and vegetables were added. In our case, once a day we were given a bowl containing a small amount of watery rice. It equated to about a quarter of a starvation diet.

Being from the city, we were not welcomed by the local population. The villagers watched us like hawks and treated us like criminals. If they caught us in any misdemeanour, they would immediately inform the soldiers and provide an excuse for some creative persecution. There were no doors on our huts and no privacy. Anyone could walk in if they felt like it, and we were spied upon at all times by both the villagers and our guards. Any conversation could be easily overheard through thin bamboo walls, so rather than speak we found it safer to live in silence for months at a time. An unguarded word or action—even a cough—would attract unwanted attention. Communication between family members was reduced to a touch rather than a hug, a glance rather than a kind word. The level of savagery dealt out by the Khmer Rouge rapidly increased. I was never sure if they were under orders, or just giving in to their most primitive instincts that found pleasure in the suffering of others. They needed little excuse to torture, maim or kill. I could not comprehend the reasons for such mindless brutality. I just tried to escape its attention.

We were told that all private property was to be confiscated, although the city people seemed to be singled out for special attention. We were called upon to renounce our individual rights by turning over all our remaining belongings, so that everything would belong to *Angkar*. All laws and orders were carried out in the name of the regime and everything from work, to sex, to family life, was tightly controlled.

The only vice permitted in the village was that people could chew the nuts of the betel tree, if they wanted to. People had to find them on their own time though, and they had precious little of that. Chewing betel nut was a fairly harmless and moderately repulsive habit, practiced by many people in Cambodia. The nuts of a specific species of palm tree were wrapped in a leaf from the betel plant that was coated with lime paste. The combination formed a mild narcotic with a similar effect to a cup of coffee. People who indulged believed that they were also protected from tooth decay, although this was difficult to prove given that the habit stained their teeth dark red. A copious amount of saliva was generated in the process, which was periodically spat onto the ground or into a spittoon. The Khmer Rouge permitted the practice partly because it kept people quiet, but mostly because the leaves and nuts grew wild in the jungle, so it would have been virtually impossible to eliminate. Mother chewed betel nut and though I did not like it, under certain circumstances it was a particularly helpful habit to cultivate.

Regardless of the consequences of being caught, Mother was not about to give up her remaining gold. She needed a hiding place, one that she had good reason to keep close at hand and one that would withstand an unexpected search. She made herself a bamboo tube that could contain rather more lime paste than was strictly necessary for the average betel nut chewer. The bamboo tube leaned against a wall in the corner of the hut and Mother never appeared to pay much attention to it. She did not want anyone suspecting that there might be more to it than met the eye. Within the first month of our arrival at the village, when no one was in the hut during the day, the Khmer Rouge soldiers came to search for anything of value. Upon our return we would often find our few possessions strewn across the floor or missing altogether; however, the worthless bamboo tube was never disturbed. Concealed at the base of the tube was Mother's horde of gold, a secret hidden right in front of everyone. A secret that would have meant her death if anyone had found it.

Sickness was endemic in the primitive conditions and Father was the first person in my family to become ill with a bout of malaria not long after we moved to the village. It is a disease something like a flu that will not go away and could lie dormant in the body, only to re-emerge months later when the immune system is otherwise occupied. Father would shiver violently and no amount of warmth or blankets could help. The spasms alternated with a burning fever that drenched his clothes with sweat. For two weeks he suffered headaches and dizziness, followed by nausea, vomiting, abdominal cramps, a dry retching cough and muscle pain. Malaria is often fatal and kills millions each year. Father was not getting better as time went on, but Mother heard that a doctor had recently come to our village.

The doctor had been expelled from a city the same as ours and she assumed that a man with a quick mind, an educated and clever man, might have some hidden supplies. She was right, although after Mother tracked him down he took some convincing that she was not a spy who would turn him in for keeping capitalist medicine. Mother could be very persuasive, however, not to mention persistent. My father was plainly not feigning his illness, so she was able to trade some of her gold for an anti-malarial injection. The injection was given to Father in the dead of night and almost certainly saved his life.

Sometime after Father's battle with malaria both Veng and Mei contracted rubella, which was common among children and easily identifiable by a high temperature and the rash that developed on their faces. Veng suffered a lot of pain and cried constantly for days. He refused to open his eyes because the gummy secretions caused by the illness had almost glued his lids shut. To keep up his strength Khay would quietly sneak away from the village to trap quail, and even more covertly cook them over an open fire. In doing this he risked severe punishment, as no food was allowed outside of the paltry offerings of the dining hall. He managed to convince his younger brother to open his eyes and eat some sweet quail meat, which cheered up Veng immensely.

Mother could not turn to the doctor for help this time because he had simply vanished one night and was never seen again. Most probably his education had been noticed and he had met his end in a shallow grave. Medicine was almost impossible to find, so we consulted a witch doctor who happened to live nearby. This individual was a woman whose only credentials appeared to be advanced age, wild hair and a disconcerting lack of teeth. Of course she had no training, skills or medical knowledge, but when people are desperate enough they often turn to nonsense, no matter how fanciful the advice might seem.

The witch doctor told Huoy to gather dried human faeces, fry it in a pan, mix the result with water and make Mei drink it. Mei did not protest although she probably should have, but she trusted her parents and drank the noxious brew. To the apparent surprise of the witch doctor, the treatment did not help at all. Next, she instructed us to wash the stairs leading up to her own hut, collect the dirty water and have Mei drink that. Again this had no effect and by now we should have suspected that something was amiss, however, in Cambodia one does not question age or authority. It simply is not done. The witch doctor then told us to crush earth worms and put them in coconut juice, again for Mei to drink. Neither patient nor worms enjoyed the experience and the 'doctor' expressed shock that this potent offering had not done the trick.

The old crone seemed nothing if not persistent. She plucked a tooth from her own jaw which was black and rotten with age and had us grind it to a fine powder. Once again this was mixed with water and drunk by Mei, who had to hold her nose against the smell. The last straw was a direction to collect and drink untreated sewage water, from where the community had been bathing and using as a toilet. Houy balked at this notion and came to the conclusion that the witch doctor was trying to kill Mei. In hindsight I realised how naive we had all been and that she had been taking advantage of our ignorance and desperation. She had enjoyed punishing us for being city people, although why she chose to take it out on a miserably sick five-year-old child was anyone's guess.

To be worth the tiny price of feeding us, we had to prove that we were serving the revolution by being productive in the fields, and work was found for everyone regardless of their physical condition. Even the oldest adults and small children were expected to labour all day, every day, even if they were capable of nothing more than collecting dried dung for fertiliser. The older children were permanently sent far away from their parents to work in other villages. Mei and Veng stayed at home; in a rare moment of common sense, *Angkar* recognised that they were too young to do even the simplest tasks. Children my age were set to work around the village at a variety of mindlessly dull jobs, and were only permitted to return to our huts after dark. Mother was assigned to work in the fields and Father worked with the older men's group.

He was given the task of weaving *prakea* baskets, which was a skill in which he had no experience and even less talent.

The Khmer Rouge said that the only thing that could prevent the purification of Cambodia was the lack of cooperation of the city people. The villagers were warned to be suspicious of us and to closely supervise our activities at all times. We were informed of this policy by some of the local children, who had not seemed to have bought into the prevailing propaganda. Plenty of the original inhabitants had, however, and with the encouragement of *Angkar* they were openly scornful of us. They seemed to me to be positively delighted to point out our shortcomings. Physical labour was very important in the new Cambodia and we lacked many, in fact most, of the necessary manual skills. No attempt was made to discover if any of the people had knowledge that could be applied in the village. We had not been relocated to teach, but rather to learn the humility that we allegedly lacked, and to be reformed through backbreaking work.

The Khmer Rouge soldiers were able to release the pent up indignation that they had been storing for a lifetime by forcing the pampered city dwellers to do the dirtiest jobs that they could think up. Their resentment had been fed by the perceived snobbishness and arrogance of the business class, but up until then they had been powerless to do anything about it. They despised people like my father in particular, because they believed that as a businessman he had made money by taking advantage of the workers. My family and people like us represented all that they envied and hated, and we had unwittingly made it easier for ourselves to be targeted.

Back in Kratie, Father had always insisted that we speak Chinese at home, and although he spoke Khmer it was with a very heavy accent. In the village it was compulsory to speak Khmer at all times and because he was easily identified as Chinese, no one outside of our family wanted to associate with him. The same went for the rest us because we all had the fair skin that comes from being *koon chen,* people of Chinese descent. Our lack of Khmer skills only added to the problem, because the local people were of pure indigenous stock, *nek moulitarn,* and did not like the Chinese one bit. Even if they had no particular view on the subject, being civil to us would put them in danger of losing their own freedom, or lives.

Father was depressed with the situation, but he kept his mouth shut and did what he was told without question or complaint. If it was not for Mother, who spoke fluent Khmer and could cover for him, Father would have quickly been on the target list of the local Khmer Rouge. In effect, if he had drawn any attention to himself he would have been a dead man.

To keep a tight rein on the population, the Khmer Rouge leaders relied heavily on *chlop,* informers to spy on the people. The spies' job was to gather whatever information they could, by whatever means they could contrive, on every member of the recently arrived city people. They snooped around at night to overhear conversations in an attempt to identify certain categories among the new arrivals. They were particularly looking for people who had worked for the government; students; the wealthy; or people who wore glasses, had soft hands or light skin. In short, they were seeking anyone who would welcome a return to the old order, anyone who might rebel against the new regime. Regardless of their actual circumstances, people with pale skin were classified as rich, and my whole family was light skinned because of our Chinese ancestry on both sides. Maintaining our distance and distrust of anyone outside of our immediate family was the only way for us to survive.

The Khmer Rouge encouraged people to dedicate themselves to the communist cause, by first promoting a carefully selected few to be group leaders then treating them favourably. They never picked the city people for these roles, but instead chose the local villagers who they rightly thought were more likely to be sympathetic to the new regime. Through no fault of their own, these people were mostly illiterate and ignorant of the world outside of their immediate location. Some of them had never travelled more than a few kilometres away from the place of their birth. They were anxious to win the favour of their new masters though, and rapidly seemed to lose any hesitation to do the various ghastly things that *Angkar* ordered.

Most of the spies were teenage children who were easily brainwashed into enjoying their newfound power. We were afraid of them because whatever these spies reported to the Khmer Rouge was believed without question, no matter how absurd the accusation. No one criticised *Angkar* in public—even the smallest snide comment could lead to arrest, detention and worse. If we had been accused of any misdemeanour then we would have been immediately sent to a *kawsang* re-education camp, from which no one ever returned. The local informants became very powerful and were always watchful for any misdeed. Any information that they could find was proudly reported to the local Khmer Rouge leader, like a cat presenting a stinking carcass to its owner as if it was a deed worthy of praise, rather than simpleminded butchery.

All of we city people had to be constantly aware of how we behaved. It was a game that we were forced to play every day, with the penalties for a wrong move ranging from the merely unpleasant to the most horrible imaginable. The informants used their power to its full *the maximum* and never seemed to think twice about the punishments that followed in their wake. They constantly tried to demonstrate that the city people were their inferiors and were wholly under their power. They really did not have to bother because we were completely at their mercy.

When I heard shouts and screams during the night, it was likely that the next day someone, or even an entire family, would be missing from the village. These people were taken away to re-education camps or killed on the spot, but in either case they were never seen alive again. The murdered victims were buried in shallow graves that were often exposed by the heavy tropical rain. Partially clothed skeletons appeared, as if trying to crawl from beneath the muddy earth, only to be gnawed at and scattered by the rats and other carrion eaters. At other times the corpses were left to bloat and rot in the jungle as a macabre example to anyone who might be entertaining impure thoughts.

As long as we kept working hard *Angkar* would tolerate us, although it was a precarious existence at best. My mother was no stranger to hard work, but she had never before been forced to labour in the rice fields from dawn until dusk. She spent every day knee deep in mud, bent over and planting rice seedlings in the flooded paddies. Mother became ill, but she forced herself to carry on because she was afraid that her group leader would accuse her of being lazy. She went on working until she became too ill to even get up from the bamboo floor of the hut where she slept. To complain was to rebel and anyone who rebelled against *Angkar* could look forward to a life that was painful and short. The Khmer Rouge did not call it murder of course. They said that anyone who rebelled would have to learn their lesson. They would be taken into the jungle to be *komtech,* a word usually applied to the disposal of bugs. It means to be smashed, destroyed.

Malnutrition started to take its toll on everyone in the village. In the past Mother had always possessed beautiful, lustrous skin and glistening black hair. I watched as months of poor quality food and too little of it made her hair go wiry and her skin dull, as she began to show the signs of starvation. Her eyes became sunken and the skin covering her arms and cheeks grew thin, seeming too large for her body, like an ill-fitting dress. Her muscles were eaten away as she continued to work for fourteen to eighteen hours a day, and her appearance mirrored the rest of us. People were already weak from malnutrition, and more became ill from the unhygienic conditions. They began to perish all around me in great numbers, sometimes before my very eyes.

So many people were disappearing, dying or being murdered that it became obvious that the population of Cambodia was on a downwards spiral. Short-sighted though they were, it occurred to *Angkar* that the country needed a steady supply of children to work the land if they were to sustain the revolution into the future. The Khmer Rouge selected young men and women to marry and effectively become breeding stock to produce the next generation. They chose the couples by whatever warped criteria they thought appropriate and announced their decision publicly. Arranged marriages had always been relatively common in Cambodia, but no one would become too upset if either of the couple strongly objected to the other. There would be an amount of shame to the families to be sure, but shots were seldom fired. In this new world the price of dissent was death, and each couple had no choice but to agree. An unsanctioned premarital affair would also end in execution if discovered, and if two people actually did want to marry then approval had to be sought from the authorities. *Angkar* periodically prepared wedding parties for one hundred couples or more, although there was little joy to be found in the events. The forced marriages were used by men in power to entrap, for themselves, girls who normally would not choose to have anything to do with them.

The days of the mass weddings were a holiday for the couples involved, though everyone else worked as usual. *Angkar* conducted the ceremonies, if you could call them that. They ordered the couples to stand and take the hand of their partner, most of them just meeting for the first time. A soldier handed each of the people a red and white chequered scarf, which served the Cambodian peasant as everything from a towel to a carrying sling. They were then declared husband and wife, with none of the traditional rituals. When the ceremony finished the couples had a banquet prepared for them, and given the dire state of their health, the extra food probably eased the way for all to go along with the process.

The weddings did not always go according to plan, and when working in a field near a mass wedding, I saw one such incident. A young woman had been chosen by a Khmer Rouge officer to be his wife. The man was an unpleasant slob even as these things went, rank with body odour and fat, while virtually everyone around him had a build somewhere between thin and skeletal. His bride to be was very pretty and thirteen years old, at most. She was also brave. When it came time to hold hands and make the marriage more or less official, she flatly refused. From my vantage point I could hear him shouting furiously, as he lost a rapidly increasing amount of face before the now motionless and silent crowd of people. Finally he seized the girl by the hair and dragged her behind a row of huts. There was a breathless pause that seemed to last forever but which must have only been a few moments, then a single shot rang out. The officer stomped out from behind the huts and brusquely motioned for the ceremony to continue without his further participation.

The couples were given a few days together, presumably in the hope that they would get on with producing some much needed children. After this brief respite they were again separated into their work groups. I did not believe that *Angkar* could succeed in its goal of *chamren pracheachun* to increase the population. Surely marriages forced upon people in such an evil manner could never last, or at least I fervently hoped not. In any event, it seemed impossible that many babies would result from the pairings. Almost all of the women's periods had stopped because of nutritional deficiency, forced labour and psychological trauma. They were no more than skin and bone.

Mother had already given birth to as many children as she was likely to, so she escaped such depredations. After months knee deep in the mud and leeches of the rice fields, she was reassigned to cook in the communal kitchen. The job of cook was much sought after because it was less physically demanding than working out in the sun. It also meant that one could eat better, if a degree of caution was observed. The cooks prepared special meals for the Khmer Rouge leaders and were permitted extra privileges, such as the freedom to leave the kitchen in order to obtain supplies. This more lenient attitude probably avoided the possibility of some form of poison finding its way into the leader's meals, at least most of the time.

The cooks were assisted by four women who worked in the dining hall and were responsible for going to the village store each day to obtain rice for the day's meal. Quantities were determined by the member of the Khmer Rouge who was in charge, and luxury foods such as chickens and ducks were reserved for the meals of Khmer Rouge officials. It was forbidden to kill an ox or a buffalo for meat, since these were needed for ploughing and transport. Every day, water had to be carried in buckets from the village well to the tank outside the dining hall. Firewood was collected from the jungle around the village.

Mother was becoming increasingly frantic in her worry about her family's health. People were dropping around us as the lack of food took its toll, but she was in the rare position of being able to do something about it. Mother began to steal rice and vegetables for us, and she knew that she was trading a slow death by starvation for the possibility of an abrupt and painful one at the hands of the Khmer Rouge if she was caught. Concealing a small amount under her clothes, Mother would bring the food back to share with us. Anything, even leftover cooked rice, was carefully collected, dried, hidden and saved for later. Most prized of all was some pig lard, because of its taste and high energy value. My father secretly cooked rice at home, topping it with the fried pork fat and a sprinkle of salt. When I came home from a day of gathering cow dung, father showed me the small metal pot, its bottom black from the fire. He lifted the lid to reveal the savoury treat inside which immediately made my stomach growl and my mouth water. I buried the spoon into the pot, shovelling the rice into my mouth. As quickly as it entered my mouth it was gone, swallowed as if I was in a contest. Once you have eaten something no one can take it away from you, and that modest portion of rice with fat and salt was the tastiest dish I had eaten since we had moved to the village.

It was not safe for my father to draw attention to himself in any way, so he remained in the background as much as possible, shuffling about his tasks with his head bowed. Khay was only ten at the time, but he took on the role of a grown man and head of the household. We would search for and dig up wild potatoes to supplement the pitiful rations that were provided at the one communal meal each day. We wandered deep into the jungle, searching the ground for small vines that blended easily into the undergrowth. The task was made all the more difficult because we had to find vines that were semi-dried, otherwise the plants were immature and there would be no potatoes underneath the ground.

On one such expedition Khay trod on a thorn with his bare foot, a mishap that was painful at the time and quickly developed into an infection. The top of his foot became swollen and turned an angry red colour. It caused him so much pain that he cried every day and we could no longer go food gathering together. Mother would boil a cloth in water and bathe his foot in order to ease the pain, but there was little else she could do. Khay's foot felt hot to the touch and he said that the pain was unbearable, which for Khay was really saying something. He suffered most during the night when there was nothing to distract him, much to the annoyance of the other people in the village. The huts were built so close to each other that there were few secrets, even if the various spies of the Khmer Rouge had not been paying attention. He scratched softly around the wound to ease the pain and Mother found some sour leaves to boil in water, so that he could submerge his foot and try to reduce the inflammation. We had already learned our lesson at the hands of the witch doctor and did not bother to consult the old crone for more dubious advice. Khay tried to cope with the excruciating pain stoically, but it did not begin to fade until two weeks later.

With their lack of education and general contempt for all things academic, the Khmer Rouge was not as organised or efficient as they might have been. They did take the trouble to maintain some records, however, and the most important of these were the death lists. These documents noted anyone who had come from the cities, as well as anyone who had caused trouble or might conceivably do so in the future. We were the city people, the new people, the weeds, *kmang,* the enemy. The village people particularly loathed anyone of Chinese descent, who they felt were responsible for forcing them into debt and then demanding crippling interest. In a country with no insurance system, social security or government bail-outs, loaning money was a risky business and this forced up interest rates. Add a canny businessman with an eye for profit, and an ill-informed borrower could quickly find themselves owing much more than they had borrowed in the first place.

The prevailing view was that Chinese people were lying, cheating, stinking thieves. Their money had been earned with the blood, sweat and tears of the poor peasant people and mere redistribution was not enough. The Khmer Rouge leadership wanted retribution and ordered a purge of Chinese people, having them tortured and buried in shallow graves, or left to rot in the jungle. Some were forced to dig their own graves as a primitive but effective form of psychological torture. The helpless victims' hands were bound behind their backs, and the shinbones and kneecaps of each leg were shattered by a wooden club. This was done in the belief that there is no greater pain that can be inflicted on a human body, without causing the victim to go into immediate shock. A quick death by heart attack would be unsatisfying to *Angkar.* There was little point in inflicting pain on a person who was no longer capable of feeling it.

The hideous acts of the Khmer Rouge were designed to intimidate the people into submission. They ripped out fingernails with pliers, or tied up the victim in the blazing sun for days, until they were literally sunburned and dehydrated to death. They whipped people until the flesh peeled from their bones, which was quickest of all and was the most common form of torture. Some of these crimes I witnessed directly, some were seen by other members of my family, and others were just whispered rumour. The Khmer Rouge was capable of anything though, and I believed them all.

The Khmer Rouge justified their actions by claiming that the Chinese had thoughts and memories that were tainted by evil Westerners. They said that we had lived off the blood and sweat of the farmers and the poor. They said that we still carried memories of the former Cambodia, memories that were corrupted by the decadence of people we had never even met. The Khmer Rouge soldiers seemed incapable of realising that they had become the thing they despised. They took what did not belong to them, the things they had not worked for. They took everything from us: our home, our family and our identities. I was eight years old and afraid of who I was. I was terrified that they would hear my thoughts, feel my anger and decide that they were better off without me. They would crush me if they knew.

In Khmer the word *kruosa* meant family, but under the rule of the Khmer Rouge it changed to mean spouse. In effect, the concept of family was redefined to exclude children altogether. Children no longer belonged to their parents; they no longer had parents at all, nor brothers or sisters. They had only *Angkar*. The Khmer Rouge told us to forget about family, and the simple human emotion of missing your brothers and sisters became a crime. We were not allowed to cry or show any grief when they took away our loved ones. They favoured some children, encouraging them to find fault with their peers. They wanted them to spy on their own parents and report back to the *meKorg*, the brigade leaders. The effect of this was as predictable as it was foul.

Schoolyard politics rapidly took over. Children took advantage of the situation to cause trouble for those whom they did not like, and if the enemy had no particular faults there was always the tactic of making up stories. In this way they tried to find favour with the brigade leaders, and never mind the consequences for the accused. Children with particularly fertile imaginations could find themselves eating at the head table alongside the commanders, with better food and plentiful rice. Others would see this and want a taste of the rewards of power, so they joined in the accusations and the cycle would continue, with the most convincing storytellers rising to the top. Children, accused by other children, were punished for real or imagined crimes. Many were sent to the re-education camps. Most never returned.

It would have been easy to condemn people for such behaviour, but I could not. They were children and until one has been truly hungry it is impossible to judge them. This was not the sort of hunger that comes after a day's hard work and carries with it the anticipation of a good meal. It was not the satisfaction of a dieter trying to lose weight, feeling the emptiness in their stomach for the first time in their pampered life and knowing that it might actually be good for them. It was the gnawing ache that comes from slaving in the hot sun for the benefit of others, knowing that the best reward one could hope for was a small bowl of thin tasteless gruel, and sometimes not even that. It was the knowledge that I did not eat yesterday and I had no reason to think that I would ever eat again.

- 7 -

Day After Day

The countryside was dotted with Buddhist temples called *wat*. To a Western observer there would have seemed to be more than could possibly be needed for the benign form of religion that Buddhism entails. It would be natural to think that in a poor country, resources could be better spent on more practical buildings. This would be to miss the fact that the temples were not just centres of worship. They were meeting places, schools, town halls, and somewhere for the elderly to go to gossip about their children, grandchildren, or whoever of their number did not happen to show up that day. The temples were among the more solidly built structures in the countryside and were soon turned into prisons by *Angkar*. The schools that were usually built alongside the temples were turned into Khmer Rouge headquarters where people were interrogated, tortured and killed. A certain status was traditionally granted to a *wat* that had a large number of statues of the Buddha adorning its walls. These figures were vandalised or destroyed as the Khmer Rouge displayed their contempt for the old order. The all too rare books that the schools contained were declared to be a corrupting influence and were burned or used for cigarette papers. The destruction of knowledge was one of the minor evils in the greater scheme of things.

Each day we tried to ignore our aches and pains in the leech infested rice fields, digging and carrying heavy baskets of dirt for hours on empty stomachs. The women, particularly those from the city, were often up to their waists in water. They were most afraid of the large leeches, which were thicker than a man's finger and infested the paddies. Slimy and persistent, they could not be felt as they attached themselves to a leg and gnawed a hole through the skin. They dropped off when satiated; leaving a trickle of blood and a wound that could become infected. Another species of leech common to the area was tiny but considered even more dangerous, for it could slip into a woman's vagina or a man's penis. There it would remain for days until it had drunk its fill, finally detaching itself and leaving of its own accord. In this worst case scenario the pain became excruciating. Everyone who worked in the fields was frequently preyed upon by the leeches.

As the sun rose to its highest point, the bell at the dining hall would ring out to the workers to signal that they were midway through another wretched day. They were now allowed to get what rest they could and dropped their baskets wherever they happened to be at the time. Everybody hurried to the dining hall along the raised dirt paths that marked the boundary of each rice field. We were ordered to walk in single file to make it easier for the Khmer Rouge to watch us, in case someone had thoughts of escape. We were all dressed alike in the black uniform with our chequered red and white *kroma* scarves wrapped around our necks or heads.

Because of the interference of the new regime, the fields were being worked by more and more people with little experience of the task. The crops were producing less than they should have, with the lion's share going to the Khmer Rouge enforcers and their favoured servants. My only possessions were a bowl and spoon with which I ate my one meal each day, squatting on the dirt floor. There was never enough and even though I ate every last morsel of what I was given, the unending sameness of my diet began to dim my spirit. When it was available the cooks would add pumpkin or sweet potatoes to the watery rice porridge. Every meal would consist of the same thing, for months on end, and I became so sick of pumpkin and sweet potatoes that, given any other choice, I never wanted to see or eat them again. Malnourishment and worm infections made my stomach swell like a balloon.

The Khmer Rouge brigade leaders set a time limit to eat before the bell rang again, and if anyone did not finish in time they lost what remained of their pathetic but precious meal. Thus I learned to eat fast. With this being the only meal of the day, everyone constantly searched for anything they could find that was edible. If they could not consume this extra food during the day, they would hide it and eat it at night after everyone was asleep. There was no thought of sharing. We were all slowly starving.

I was assigned to collect cow dung and to chop up weeds to use for fertiliser. There was nothing else to do and nowhere to go. If there was a reason to leave the village for a short time, a permit from *Angkar* was needed. Approval was rarely given unless there was something in it for the person in authority. There were no weekends, holidays, or any kind of celebration. We were told that such things were at best unnecessary and at worst corrupting.

The Khmer Rouge had taken over every village by then, setting down arbitrary rules and regulations along the way. They investigated families for any signs of disloyalty or resistance and took children aside to ask them to talk about their parents. An innocent statement by a three-year-old could rapidly escalate into a capital offence, especially if an example was deemed necessary. They hid under the huts at night to eavesdrop on families who thought they were speaking in private. Families who stayed together drew a certain strength and support from each other, so the Khmer Rouge sought to separate and isolate them. Children as young as five were torn from their parents and sent to different labour camps. Cambodians of all races and classes worked without wages or respite, on projects in which they had no say.

- 8 -

The Blindfold

After about six months in the new village, my family was again split up and relocated according to sex and age. This was done to prevent us from forming relationships with each other, to keep us off balance and under control. Such people would have no one to turn to but *Angkar*—a huge family that could only be considered ideal to someone who had been thoroughly brainwashed. Only the youngest children were allowed to stay with their parents. I was taken away while the twins Mei and Veng were allowed to remain with Mother and Father, though this did not last for long. As soon as they were five years old they too were mature enough to be sent to the work camps. Only the very old remained in the village.

One camp consisted of single women and another contained just the single men. Married men and women were also segregated, and if a woman had a new baby to care for then they were put into yet another camp. All of the children who were five or older were sent far away from their parents to labour camps, one for each sex and age group. Khay went to a male *kong koma* children's labour camp. My sisters Keang, Bouy and Houy were close enough in age to go to the same female *kong chalet* youth labour camp. The twins Mei and Veng were of course the same age, but they were brother and sister so they were separated for the first time in their lives. I was sent to a children's labour camp on my own to join dozens of other eight-year-old girls.

My oldest brother Huor was the only exception. He had always been quite a thoughtful person, which did not go well with the brigade leaders. He was found reading a Chinese story book while he was meant to be watching a herd of cows. It was bad enough that he was not looking after *Angkar's* valuable property with sufficient zeal, but reading a book—and a *Chinese* book at that? He was sent straight to prison and was lucky he wasn't shot on the spot.

My assignment to the camp marked my total separation from my family with complete finality. From that time on I was no longer under the care or protection of anyone in my family and was now utterly at the mercy of the young Khmer Rouge *meKorg* brigade leader. I had to address the Khmer Rouge regime as *Angkar*, as if it was my sole parent and everything I owned belonged to *Angkar*. This was no great loss; it had been some time since I had owned anything at all. Clothing of any colour other than black was prohibited. The Khmer Rouge brigade leaders wore black pyjama-like uniforms, sandals made of old car tyres and red and white chequered *kroma* scarves. The Chinese-made AK-47 assault rifles slung over their shoulders backed up their authority. That particular weapon was prized for its simplicity, reliability, firepower, and the fact that it was light enough to be used by small children.

By the time I got to the camp there were already many children who were about my age. We had to address each other as *met*, a word that meant 'comrade'. The Khmer Rouge brigade leader took me to a long shack made of bamboo with a roof of thatched palm leaves and assigned me a place to sleep. She told us not to love our parents because they were not the ones who now supported us and so we could not depend on them. She told us to love the Khmer Rouge brigade leaders and to work hard so that our country could be prosperous. Though she was not much older than me, obedience was guaranteed by our fear of the gun that she carried on her shoulder all day. She never worked at all, but stood watching and pointing her finger at whatever she wanted done, all the while shouting at us to work harder. She did not contribute anything of value, but she ate better food than the rest of us and more of it. At meal times she sat at a different table with the other brigade leaders. To me she was the personification of the evil that had overtaken my country.

Our *meKorg* brigade leader's voice was annoying and she looked mean to me, a first impression that hardly did her justice. She was always ordering everyone around and obviously could not stand the sight of us. She regarded us with the disdain usually reserved for cockroaches. Needless to say, I did not like her at all. She was round of face, thin, short, dark-skinned, and in far better condition than the children she oversaw. She was from a poor indigenous family and clearly enjoyed her new position of power. She was brutal towards us and delighted in keeping everyone working continuously, regardless of whether there was anything useful to be done. She yelled constantly, in a world where politeness had become a thing of the past.

There was no reward for obeying other than to avoid the consequences of not doing so. If we did not do as we were told we received a severe beating as punishment. It was a carrot and stick approach without the carrot. The leaders made us cheer and chant that we respected and loved working hard for *Angkar*. All I could think about was my family and how much I missed them. Being away from Mother made me cry every night, but quietly, so that the brigade leaders would not hear and make an example of me for my weakness. They had made it abundantly clear that they would beat an eight-year-old girl for crying over her lost mother.

Each morning we were woken at 5am by a bell rung with great enthusiasm by our brigade leader. She would stand at the end of the shack yelling at us to get up, striding among the sleepy children and kicking ribs or yanking us to our feet if we did not respond quickly enough. She was always bright eyed and well rested, which was probably a result of having done nothing the previous day except watch us work and pass judgment on our misdeeds. Everyone, even the many sick children, had to line up every day for inspection by our brigade leaders. It was at this inspection that our brigade leaders decided who was well enough to work in the fields and who was not. Those who were sufficiently ill were allowed to rest, but their already meagre food rations were cut by half. The Khmer Rouge referred to anyone pretending to be sicker than they were as a feverish rabbit. Beyond the food reduction, it did not pay to gain a reputation as a malingerer. There was no form of medical attention so we got well by ourselves, or died by ourselves.

We were forced to march many kilometres to whichever worksite we were assigned to that day. At first I was again ordered to pick up dried cow manure for fertiliser. There was no end to the crap for me to pick up and the task seemed to follow me wherever I went. I carried a basket against my hip and walked through the fields from sunrise to sunset, seven days a week, searching for the smelly lumps. At my age I should have been attending school and living at home with proper food to eat. Instead, I was forced to sleep on the ground and work twelve hours a day come rain or shine. Contrary to popular belief, the tropical rains are neither cooling nor soothing when you are underfed and without shelter. I was constantly just plain wet, cold and miserable.

According to the brigade leaders our duty as daughters of *Angkar* was solely to work hard, and they followed us all the time to make sure we did just that. As it turned out there are worse jobs than picking up cow and buffalo dung. As a change of pace, we were sometimes ordered to repair dams and build paddy dykes. Work was entirely by hand and no machines of any kind were used on brigade worksites. We rarely even had hand tools and repaired rice paddy dykes by scooping up mud with our bare hands and depositing it where it was needed. For a child, playing in the mud is grand fun until they realise that they will be doing it all day, every day, with no end in sight.

Occasionally we were lucky and given a hoe to help with the digging, but this carried with it a risk. We had to take great care not to dig too hard or the handle might break, and whoever was using it at the time would be subject to severe criticism. Absurd as it was, a broken stick marked us as enemies of the state. Everyone had to work hard for fear of punishment by the brigade leaders. Poor work meant that *prachum khosang* education meetings were called to deliver a bout of prolonged and abusive criticism, which also meant that everyone missed their sleep. We were encouraged to take out any frustration we felt on the child who had broken *Angkar's* tools.

Never in my life had I been forced to labour so hard and for so long, moving through a fog of exhaustion before each day was over. Planting rice fields was no better. It involved less heavy lifting but we spent the entire day hunched over to stick the seedlings into the mud and shuffling backwards so as not to trample the young plants. Even if we got used to this uncomfortable position, we never got used to the huge leeches that swam through the murky water searching for blood.

At noon the bell rang again for our one meal of the day and everyone hurried from the fields into the lines to wait for their portion of gruel. Hygiene was poor and flies gathered in swarms so that I had to constantly wave one hand to keep flies from settling on my lips. The sick children ate separately, but instead of being given better quality or extra food in order to regain their strength, they received less. The constant refrain was that those who do not work do not eat. Of course this meant that those who were sick still tried to work in order to keep receiving their normal rations. People at the end of their physical limits were more susceptible to disease and many who fell sick never recovered. After the usual ten minutes to eat what little we were given, we were sent back out into the burning sun or the pouring rain to work until nightfall.

Children all around me began to die of disease, abuse and malnutrition. In due course the parents would simply be informed that their child was dead, if they were told at all. If they wept or showed any signs of grief, they were reprimanded for indulging in bourgeois individualistic sentimentality. They were told that their children had died for the revolution. They were told that they should be proud, not sorrowful, and determined to strive even harder to give more to *Angkar*. The same attitude would be directed towards a wife showing sorrow over the execution of her husband. Anyone who was executed was an enemy. They must have been, we were told—why else would they have been executed? Expressions of sorrow for the death of such people indicated a failure to love *Angkar*. This was a serious crime in itself, so people suppressed their real feelings. This attitude reached insane heights when even the killing of the blameless was excused as necessary. It was said to be better to execute many innocents than to let a single guilty person live.

I cannot say that any of my co-workers were my friends. I could not take the risk of befriending and opening up to anybody for fear that whatever I talked about might be used against me. I was from the city and also of Chinese descent, which placed me somewhere just above the leeches on the social order. If I was noticed by the brigade leader or her flunkies, my origins would have been used as an excuse to persecute me. Fears such as this kept everyone else from questioning the new order and made sure they stayed under control. I was only dimly aware of this at the time, but I knew that my family's origins would attract the sort of attention that could get us punished or killed. I instinctively kept my head down, my gaze averted and my mouth shut.

The brigade leaders told us that *Angkar* was ever watchful, that they were like a pineapple, with eyes everywhere that saw everything. Not even the smallest indiscretion would escape their notice, and they often came to take children away during the night. Arrests were made for no apparent reason and the victims were marched off into the forest, where they were usually clubbed to death with a hoe to save the price of a bullet. Their bodies were buried in shallow graves or left to lie where they fell, as a reminder to the rest of us. Before the Khmer Rouge I had never seen a dead person before. I almost passed out the first time I saw a body in the jungle, bloody from having been beaten to death. The second time, I got a splitting headache and could feel my heart racing in my chest. By the time I was nine years old I was well accustomed to the sight and smell of death, but I never got used to it.

As an eight-year-old, I had no sense of time and all I knew for the next four years was hunger and death. The days passed as excruciatingly slowly as they always do for a child who wishes they were elsewhere. All I cared about was food, but to ask for more was to be ungrateful. It was seen as criticism of the generosity of *Angkar* for what had been given. Whenever my stomach was empty, which was almost always, I looked at the other children's food like a predator eyeing its prey. In my life before this madness, I had been sheltered and well provided for. Hunger had never before entered my mind. Now that the memory of my family was fading, hunger was all I could think about.

I could not protest to *Angkar* and I tried to put my hunger out of my mind. Unfortunately, my stomach had ideas of its own and constantly protested to me that it needed more food. I was hungry all the time and had to be constantly on the lookout, scavenging for any additional food that I could find. I ate crickets, rice field crabs, snakes and grasshoppers. I scrambled after frogs, centipedes, scorpions and tadpoles. I no longer had any sense of revulsion and a bug in the dirt was a buried treasure to be prized. I ate rotten leaves if there was nothing else to keep the hunger pangs at bay. Once I was hungry enough, a threshold was crossed and caution was abandoned. It did not matter if an unfamiliar plant might be poisonous. If I ate it and did not die then I would live for another day. I never consumed anything that did more than make me sick, but many children around me were not so lucky and they died because of their desperation.

Each night before we were allowed to sleep, and occasionally at random times during the day, we had to attend *prachum* meetings called *khosang,* which meant to criticise. They consisted of diatribes that could last hours, during which slogans exulting *Angkar* were repeated over and over again. They told us that they wanted to build a new country and that we children were the future of *Angkar* and the future of the country. No discussion was permitted. No alternative views could be put. Meetings were even held in the rain to discuss the day's work and to criticise poor performance. This was where the Khmer Rouge pointed out our faults. Apparently we had many.

We were forced to publicly detail the sins we had committed. I frequently admitted to being a little bit lazy, to having been able to work harder, to having talked too much. None of these things were the least bit true, but if I did not admit to something the brigade leader would feel it necessary to force a confession from me, or manufacture a crime out of thin air. This could have dire consequences if she worked herself into a self-righteous frenzy and slowed the meeting down, making us miss more badly needed sleep. I learned that it was better to admit some trivial fault, accept the reprimand and be done with it as quickly and painlessly as possible. It was my policy to work hard and not to talk at all, if possible, in order to escape attention. Even if I had worked as hard as I could, I would never say so. No work was ever perfect because according to *Angkar* it was always possible to do better. Everyone was told simply that they must work harder, produce more and love *Angkar*. I had to adapt to the situation in order to survive.

Every night a person was chosen to take the brunt of the leaders' collective wrath, selected for some failing or at random if necessary. They would get everyone to point and yell at the person being criticised, even if it was a family member. They made the selected victim sit inside a circle of people who would then take turns delivering *khosang* (criticism). People would go along with this, grateful for the moment that they were not in the circle themselves. Of course everyone ended up the centre of unwanted attention sooner or later and was used as an example of a disloyal citizen.

We were told that these comrades had betrayed *Angkar* and that they needed to be *komchat* (eradicated). At the end of every meeting, we would have to recite a phrase which went along the lines of: '*The Khmer Rouge is good; they will protect us. Cheyo victory to democratic Kampuchea and parachey defeat to America.*' We would punch our fists into the air when praising *Angkar* and towards the ground when condemning America. We hated the imperialists with the passion of ignorance, heedless of the fact that no one in the camp had ever met or even seen an American. The message was easy to sell, given the B-52 air strikes that had blasted the countryside for so long.

I had not been at the camp long before I saw exactly what the Khmer Rouge was capable of when they suspected disobedience. We were ordered to a meeting thinking that it would be the usual finger-pointing rant, someone would be harangued at length and we would finally return to our shacks to sleep on the dirt floor. Instead, a child was shoved into the dimly lit circle of deathly silent girls, her eyes covered by her own red checked scarf that was tied about her head. The brigade leaders told us that she had betrayed *Angkar*. They told us that we must give everything we had for the common good. They told us that what was about to happen would befall anyone who defied them. They smashed her knees with a wooden club and she fell to the ground with a scream of agony that gradually faded to a whimper. Her splintered bones cut through her skin and blood pooled on the ground. They made sure we were all still watching before using the club to crush the back of the little girl's skull. She was eight years old. Just like the rest of us.

- 9 -

Utopia

The days were hot and monotonous but there were few complaints. No one dared to object to anything we were told to do. After some months I was moved again, this time to a new camp that was carved out of virgin forest. It was part of a plan to extend the area under cultivation and increase rice production. The new camp aimed to firstly become self sufficient and then to produce a surplus which would go to the state. The future for the permanent inhabitants of the village was to spend the rest of their lives as the poorest of peasant farmers. Their standard of living would be maintained by their Khmer Rouge masters at no more than a subsistence level. All of these new villages were established by the evacuees from provincial towns. The amount of work needed determined the length of time the labourers stayed in one location, before moving on to a different work site. As soon as one project was finished, the brigade was assigned to another.

At harvest time we moved from village to village to help wherever we were needed most. People died from a combination of exhaustion and malnutrition. We slept lined up like sardines on the dirt floor, with only a hessian rice bag for a blanket if we were lucky. The bags smelled after years of use, and mine was stained and falling apart. We could never wash them but at night

I would crawl into mine and curl up, using my *kroma* scarf as an extra cover and my spare uniform if it was dry enough. We were at the mercy of all sorts of crawling insects that would invade the hut every night, looking for food. Sometimes I was woken by a horrible pain because an ant had found its way inside my ear and bitten the tender skin. Lice took advantage of the fact that we were crammed in so close together and infested each and every one of us. I managed to borrow a lice comb to get rid of some of the pests but they always came back in a matter of days. Worst of all were the rats, which crawled over children too exhausted to notice. I became aware of the bold rodents when I was woken from sleep by the pain of a sharp teeth gnawing on my bare toes.

The Khmer Rouge brigade leaders slept in their hammocks high above us, away from the biting insects and rats. When I needed to use the toilet at night, I had to yell out my name and that I was going outside to relieve myself. After I finished, I had to call out that I was now back in line. The guards walked around with flashlights performing a head count several times each night. They made no attempt to be quiet so that the tired children could sleep undisturbed. Sometimes the Khmer Rouge brigade leaders took children out into the night. They marched them outside and they never came back.

Every morning the bell rang to wake us before the sun rose over the horizon. We grew more and more tired and some children did not get up quickly enough to satisfy the brigade leaders. They would yank us into the air by our feet and drop us onto the hard ground, threatening to beat us if we did not move more quickly. We went to work with no food in our stomachs unless we had hidden some food the day before, or could find something during the morning. We helped to grow what seemed to be a mountain of food and in return they gave us almost nothing.

We were separated from our families but we would often see the adult brigades doing heavy work that the children were not strong enough to perform. They were no better off than we were and also worked from dawn to dusk on one small meal a day. I was in the fields working one day when I saw a woman from the adult labour group resting for a moment on the rice field dyke. There were buffalo nearby and she somehow attracted the attention of one of them. Buffalo can be ill tempered at times, and this one was in a particularly bad mood. It charged at her and dug its horns deep into her stomach, lifting her into the air. Other adults ran to her aid and after a struggle they managed to pull her off the buffalo's horn. Her intestines were hanging out of the bleeding wound but all they had to bandage her injury with was her own red scarf. She was carried away and I never found out what became of her, but I cannot imagine that she survived.

Injury, illness and death were commonplace and made my wishes to be with my family all that much stronger. I had not seen any of them for two years, and had to put them out of my mind in order to concentrate on survival. My muffled feelings were due for a shock though, as one day while I was bent over in a cassava field pulling weeds, I thought I heard my name being whispered. I looked up and froze for a moment when I saw my mother just five metres away. My cry of delight died on my lips as I remembered that displays of emotion were dangerous, and that we would both be punished if caught. I wanted to run to her, to hug her, but I could not. We kept working and in a few hushed words she told me that she had been in the area, and had never given up looking for her children.

Mother asked me if I was okay, if I was getting enough to eat and if anyone was giving me any trouble. I replied that I was fine, fed and treated fairly well, all of which she no doubt knew were lies. I didn't want her to worry, and in any case there was nothing she could do to help her daughter. We had risked enough and she started to work her way away from me. I kept sneaking glances in her direction as she neared the edge of the field, and I stood a moment to pretend to stretch and see her one last time. But she was gone.

The working conditions got worse and worse, especially when our leaders took it into their heads that we should compete with other brigades. They sought the approval of their upper leadership—for this was the only currency that had any meaning in their isolated world view. The long days of forced labour took their toll and illness began to increase. Malaria was endemic to the area and was bad enough, but something as simple as diarrhoea can kill a child from dehydration within a matter of hours. The brigade leader was meant to be responsible for our welfare, but she was actually only interested in us when we were strong enough to make her look good to her superiors. If we were weak, we were useless to her.

I picked up an infection in my eyes, an inflammation I had suffered from before. It was conjunctivitis, which causes a discharge of sticky pus. My eyelids were hard to open in the morning and the eyelashes seemed glued together. I had nothing to treat myself with beyond regular bathing in unclean water. It was hard to see and I had to squint painfully under the harsh sun. I was afraid of what would happen to me if I could not work. I knew that I could fall into a downward spiral, becoming even weaker when my food ration was cut. I had seen this happen to other children often enough. Using a half-remembered remedy that I had heard somewhere, I used my own urine to bathe my eyes. The infection went away, which I felt put me one up on the witch doctors.

Months passed in the camps and it was the same routine every day. Work, work and more work. We no longer had any identity. The very words we used were altered and twisted and we were not allowed to use certain phrases that came from the city. The Khmer Rouge did not allow us to own money or personal possessions of any kind. They ruled our appearance, requiring women to wear their hair short. Cambodian culture had always placed great value on the beauty of long hair for women. Now our hair was cut at the level of our earlobes. A coconut shell was placed over our heads and any hair that showed below the edge of the shell was crudely cut away. It looked like the handiwork of a child. The head is the most sacred part of the body to a Cambodian. To be struck on the skull, or even to have a younger person touch your head is enormously insulting.

The demand for uniformity extended from the people's dress to the very landscape, and there seemed to be only one exception to the rule. Some people were given new scarves that were blue instead of red and these were clearly visible across the fields. I thought they were pretty and asked a girl who was a similar age to me if she wanted to trade. Of course she did not accept the offer since her scarf was new and mine was most certainly not. I asked the other girls what I had to do to also be rewarded, but no one knew.

My life had no significance to their great communist nation, and they told us that we were of no benefit to the country. If we died it was no loss at all. A man would be shot if he lost an ox that he was assigned to tend. A woman would be killed if she was too tired to work. The meetings every night, where we took turns finding fault with each other, were designed to reinforce the message that the individual did not matter. There was only *Angkar*.

I wish I could say that I stood up to them. I wish that I was the plucky kid who protected the weak, defied unjust authority and made those bastards back down with the sheer force of my will. I wish I had been in some Hollywood version of the world where such things were possible. People like to think that one person can change the world if only they are brave and strong enough. There had been people in Cambodia who believed that, and they were the first to die.

I survived by becoming the thing that I hated. I stole, I cheated and I lied. I did not know why the Khmer Rouge despised us so much. They seemed to have no sense of what it was to be human at all. They tortured and killed people and apparently they enjoyed doing it. They taught children to hate their parents, in some cases brainwashing them into believing that their own mother and father were their enemies. Some children were persuaded to kill their own families as the ultimate act of loyalty to *Angkar*.

By this time it had been almost three years since I had been separated from my family. We were kept on the move from camp to camp, one week in the fields and the next in the depths of the jungle. I think that they did this to disorient us, to make us so confused that we could not run back towards home or our families, even if we were willing to take the chance. Some children escaped and tried to reach their parents back in the villages. They were captured, tied up, beaten and brought back to work. We worked all day, every day under the sun, in the rain or by moonlight. They said they were creating a utopian nation where everyone would be equal. They lied of course. The whole nation was poor, but even so there was comfort to be had, if you could achieve the right position. While most of the population was dying of starvation and disease, the Khmer Rouge was creating a new upper class. It was made up of those people who had traditionally had little power and also possessed the stomach to brutalise their fellow humans. They were able to choose any woman or man they wanted to marry and they had plenty of food, Western medicine, cars and motorcycles. All the things they had taken from us.

It was not a good idea to ponder such things, but there was nothing else to think about as the hours blurred one into the next. Near the end of a long day in the fields, I was overcome by a feeling of hopelessness that dropped me to my knees. What was the good of going on if this was all I had to look forward to for the rest of my life? Maybe it was better to run right now and be cut down by the guns of the Khmer Rouge. I would finally be able to rest, one way or the other. Something wriggled in the dirt in front of me, and I saw that it was one of the spiders that had often been a meal for me. The creature had been involved in some sort of mishap and was struggling gamely along, minus two and a half legs. I considered the spider's plight and decided that if this tiny animal could continue on regardless of the odds, then so could I. My mother at least was still alive, and maybe the rest of my family was too. I got to my feet, stretched my spine and went back to work.

- 10 -

Water

We found ourselves in yet another camp, this one in a stretch of large rice paddies. As usual I had no idea where we were or what the place was called. Only the steady addition of similarly aged children kept our numbers more or less constant. Without this, the original hundred and fifty would have diminished until our brigade leader had to perform some work herself, and that would not have done at all. The rice fields were divided by innumerable dykes into squares forty metres on a side. A large irrigation canal *prek* was dug around each area, surrounding a hundred paddy fields. Control of water had always been crucial. Paddy fields were bounded by low walls of mud and the water levels were carefully manipulated to obtain the best result from the growing plants. This was not a task one could do alone, and the brigade leaders insisted that the paddies be both square and identical in size wherever possible.

The countryside all looked very attractive, especially when planted with young green rice that looked like a neatly kept lawn from a short distance away. The effort to produce such uniformity, though, was incredible. It was all done by hand, with a few simple tools and the sweat of thousands of people. There were no pumps available and the water in the paddies had to be raised by a foot-powered contraption. Before the new rice could even be planted we had to pull the old rice stems out by the roots, beating them against our thighs to knock the dirt off. From above we must have looked like a line of industrious ants; all the same size and colour with skinny arms clawing at the earth. Waiting to be crushed underfoot.

May was the monsoon season. Torrents of water poured from the sky like an infinite waterfall almost daily. My body was reduced to skin and bones and when it rained I shivered. I felt like a paper cut-out that could be easily blown over by the wind. There was no escape from the work, which continued no matter the conditions. Twelve hours a day or more on an empty stomach, until I felt that my sanity was in danger. The fields flooded and turned into shallow lakes, teeming with life. The croaking of frogs and chirping of various insects produced a melodic harmony. As long as they could stay out of reach of the starving workers they, at least, were free.

We were ordered to clear the fields and channels of floating weeds that could choke the young rice plants, wading in water up to our chests. We had to avoid the snakes, ants and scorpions that clung to the weeds in a futile attempt to stay dry. I tied my pants at the knee and waist to keep the leeches out; the water swarmed with the horrible black creatures and they never gave up for a minute. Only the fact that I was constantly knee deep in mud kept them off my feet and shins. At the end of the day when I finally got out of the water I could see the slimy spots where the leeches had tried to attach themselves to my pants. One of the other girls from my brigade was not as careful or lucky as I was, and a leech found its way into her vagina. Once there it wormed its way deep inside, becoming impossible to force out without medical instruments.

She was told to sit naked from the waist down over a pool of cow blood so that the leech could smell the blood. With luck the leech would be persuaded to leave of its own accord. I never found out if the leech cooperated because we were moved yet again the following day. I did not think I would ever lose my fear of the slimy blood suckers.

I helped to produce the new rice plants, scattering the grain kept from the last harvest into shallow paddies to grow into seedlings. When they had grown halfway to my knee we pulled them from the water, tying them into bundles and cutting off the top third, ready for transplanting. Then we had to push the seedlings, about ten at a time, deep into the mud of the prepared fields, walking backwards a step at a time to avoid crushing the new plantings. As the rice began to grow and mature it became very attractive to flocks of hungry birds and would remain so until it was harvested. We were now assigned to mind the rice fields, making noises and doing whatever we could to frighten the birds away from the ripening rice.

The fields began to turn golden and the heads of rice weighed down the stalks. In the early morning light I could see adults heading out to harvest paddies that were ready. From my point of view, it looked as though their heads were floating over the rice stalks. I wondered if Mother was with them. The birds were always up and flying at the crack of dawn, and they soared over the fields until they selected one and came swooping down to feast. As soon as they began to descend, the children whose fields were being invaded raced along the raised dykes towards the birds, shouting and waving their arms. Working as an animated scarecrow was not too demanding and was certainly better than some of the other jobs I had done. I made extra noise by clapping two lengths of bamboo together and making a sharp crack, which sent the birds on their way. They would give me a moderately annoyed look, before taking off to fly to another field. The children guarding that field would repeat the performance and so it would go; the birds hopping from field to field and back again in a cycle that paused at night, but did not end until every last stalk of rice had been harvested.

In the harvesting season the adults had to do the heavy work of cutting and stacking the rice into sheaves. These were carried on the heads of the women back to a central processing area. We children had to glean the fields afterwards, picking up any rice stalks or heads of grain that the adults had dropped as the plants were cut. By the time the rice had been harvested the fields were no longer muddy and under water. They had dried completely under the sun and the rice stalks were stiff and sharp enough to cut our bare feet, even though our skin was now tough and leathery. Apart from the stubble jabbing into our feet, this was a pleasant duty as far as we were concerned. The brigade leaders could not be bothered walking all the way over to each of us in order to check that we were picking up each and every grain. The constant threat of punishment meant that we did a tolerably good job nonetheless.

The rice grains were separated from the stalks by hand; machines that made life easier were a memory that grew increasingly distant. A circle of women or men would work to thresh the rice by day and night. There was never a mixed group because the camps were still separated along gender lines, and *Angkar* did not allow distractions. There was no let-up for either the adults or the children until the harvest was complete. The working day was extended, with an extra session starting at 7pm and lasting well into the night. After dark the field workers could not see to cut the rice so they had to help with processing the grain. The scene would be lit by the moon or a single kerosene lamp at the centre of a circle of twenty sweating people, always under the watchful eyes of the brigade leaders.

The method to release the rice from the head of the plant was to use two sticks connected by a rope, which was twisted around the base of the stalks to hold them firm. The bundle was then thrashed against an angled board which knocked the grain off the head and into a pile in the middle. The threshing was done in a confined area to avoid losing any rice or bran, and the air was thick with dust and chaff which got into our eyes and throats. After the last grains were gathered, the rice was transported by ox cart to the village rice store. Seeing so much food caused hunger pains that had to be endured without complaint. Even during the harvest, our meal was always the same small portion of rice porridge with a little salt. While processing the rice we were waist deep in food and yet starving to death.

After the rice was threshed, husked and polished, the army trucks arrived to take most of it away. I felt helpless and cheated as the vehicles carrying the big bags of grain disappeared into the distance. We had worked so hard and for so long to grow that food and it should have been *ours*! Our anger did not matter to *Angkar* and the precious rice was exported to China in exchange for armaments. The brigade leader told us that most of the rice was sent to people in battlefields who were fighting for the *padewat* revolution. When the grain left behind proved to be insufficient to last until the next harvest, we were told that it was because we had not worked hard enough. There was a certain irony in the fact that the ethnic Chinese in Cambodia were being worked to death in order to purchase the means of their oppression from their own homeland.

Although the main preoccupation of the Khmer Rouge brigade leaders was to grow rice to trade for their weapons, some infrastructure had to be maintained. Not even the most amateur civil engineer was involved. Western science and technology were condemned as bourgeois learning. Trained Cambodian engineers were enemies who had been exterminated or hid their skills for fear of their lives. Dams were constructed without the use of instruments, by men learning as they went, with no technical training and virtually no tools. An ounce of common sense would have told them that a trial and error approach would result in a massive amount of wasted effort, but ideology ruled all. Water failed to flow in irrigation canals that had an insufficient gradient and dams crumbled into rubble.

During the monsoon season it rains heavily, as any two-year-old child in Cambodia can tell you. We were woken by the bell and shouted curses in the middle of the night to repair a *tomnop teuk* dam that was about to burst. We walked barefooted and single file through the jungle for two hours, our way lit by spluttering torches made of palm leaves and tar which produced light and smoke in equal measure. The repair crew consisted only of my brigade: a hundred and fifty skinny, sleepy, ten-year-old girls. Halfway there the rain returned, together with enough thunder and lightning to wake us properly. We patched the dam by collecting rocks and mud, standing in a row to pass the material along. The shoddy wall loomed over us, taller than a house and holding back a massive volume of water. I did not think about it at the time, but if that dam had given way every one of us ten-year-old girls would have drowned or been dashed to death on the rocky river bed.

The long hours of hard work combined with a lack of proper food and medical attention meant that illness, particularly malaria, became increasingly common. If someone was infected there was nothing to do but to let the disease take its course. The local traditional remedies made little impression, and modern medicine was banned by the Khmer Rouge. The children were especially vulnerable but they were considered expendable by their overlords. I was frequently sick and had no one to care for me, so I had to learn to take care of myself. I was already thin and weak, but in no worse condition than the other girls in my brigade.

I became very ill when malaria finally found its way into my body via the tiny sting of a mosquito, the most dangerous animal to humans that the earth has ever known. It had been three years since effective medicines could be found on the black market. Even back then, few people had been willing to part with what was a rare and valuable possession. Now it was impossible to find Western drugs, unless you were one of the Khmer Rouge leaders. I came down with a burning fever that made me shake furiously, my body feeling as hot as fire. Soon after that I would be shivering with a cold that seemed to seep from inside my body, even though the day was warm. It could have been worse; some people had dysentery as well, which combined uncontrollable diarrhoea with a debilitating fever and an inability to move. They lay shivering in puddles of their own piss and shit.

To make up for the lack of modern medicines, desperate people resorted to traditional remedies. These included the use of certain leaves, roots and bark, which were said to be part of the ancient folk pharmacopoeia of the Cambodian people. They took the form of small black pills and were manufactured in the country villages. I was given some of the pills which were known as 'rabbit droppings'. They lived up to their names as far as the taste went and had no effect at all as far as I could tell. At least they did not smell like crushed cockroaches.

- II -

Bouy

By late 1978 cracks were beginning to show in the cruel regime. It was inevitable that the mindless violence could not last forever, that sooner or later help would arrive or the country would simply collapse. The Khmer Rouge responded with even more brutality. The 'new people', the city people, were searched out and targeted. They searched for people who wore glasses, whose hands were smooth and whose skin was pale because they had not spent their lives labouring under the sun. *Angkar* persecuted people with *yuon* Vietnamese blood, who they believed were *kmang*— the enemy of Cambodia. There were no trials; people were guilty solely because of who they were. Many were wrongly accused because of the way they looked, and condemned because of their heritage.

It was then that the meaning of the pretty blue scarves became clear. They were a marker to make it easier to single out those who had long ago been marked for execution. They were gathered together and told that they were being moved to a place that needed their labour. They were marched away into the night. Before they were butchered, these innocents were forced to dig pits to act as their own graves. I tried not to picture what was happening. I tried not to think of the sense of hopelessness that must have lain over the scene as dozens of ragged, wretched people scraped at the earth with their bare hands.

They knew what was about to happen. They knew that there was no escape. If they ran for the jungle they would succeed only in giving the guards target practice. By cooperating they could cling to the few minutes of life they had left. The soldiers tied the arms of their victims behind their backs and ordered them to kneel near the edge of the pits. The Khmer Rouge leaders said that a firing squad was a waste of bullets, so the condemned were killed by blows to the backs of their heads. It was quick if they were lucky, but I think by then good fortune had long since left my homeland.

During the killings I heard screams that echoed through the jungle, cries of agony that faded to a dull moaning and finally silence. They were sounds that will haunt me for the rest of my life—a person begging for their life after their bones had been smashed by the uncaring brigade leaders. They were sounds that most people have heard only from the comfort of a movie theatre seat. Imagine the worst sound you can possibly think of. Imagine it coming from your husband or wife, your daughter or son.

Bodies were piled into the pits, one on top of the other. Dirt was shovelled into the pits to cover the crime. I think that the Khmer Rouge knew that what they were doing was wrong, that this was not the act of anyone that deserved to call themselves human. During the day the heat of the sun pierced through the soil covering the mounds of bodies, brewing a stench of death that saturated the fields.

The abuse that was directed towards the inhabitants of the camps was not all one way. The paranoia of *Angkar's* upper leadership had no limits, and no one was immune. As the productivity of the land declined there were periodic spasms of violence that were, for a change, visited upon the brigade leaders. They were rounded up, seemingly at random, and themselves taken into the jungle where they were forced to confess to some imagined disloyalty. In reality they deserved death for any number of real crimes, but it was a roundabout sort of justice.

Despite the warnings and threats, the brutal torture and public executions, many people did try to escape. The choice was one between a slow and painful death from disease and starvation, or a quick and even more painful death at the hands of the Khmer Rouge if they were caught. Many people were paralysed by the fact that their families were still under *Angkar's* rule. Their responsibilities to their spouses and children kept them bound to the area they had been sent. They did not know if their loved ones were alive but they could hope. The sheer distance to be covered prevented more from making the attempt. For the people in provinces far from the Thai border, escape was practically impossible. Those who tried their luck headed for Thailand or Vietnam.

My health was getting worse as my body began to fail under the onslaught of disease, work and starvation. I developed a disease which caused oedema throughout my body. Oedema is a build-up of fluid in the body's tissues and usually occurs in the feet, ankles and legs, but in my case it spread to my entire body, causing my eyes to nearly squeeze shut. My skin inflated with fluid until it seemed ready to burst through the skin and I looked like a poorly constructed inflatable doll. When I pressed the skin in an attempt to shift the fluid, the skin would stay depressed for many seconds before slowly puffing up again. I was given some of the useless rabbit pills made from tree bark and honey, and left to live or die. I knew that if any of us became sick too often then we would be judged to be more trouble than we were worth and would disappear for good. I endured, eventually recovered, and returned to work.

It was time for the rice harvest again and with the naivety of any eleven-year-old, I hoped for a bigger food ration. There was rice being processed and loaded onto trucks by the tonne wherever I looked. Only a few years ago I would not have viewed a pile of grain with such longing. Now I had fantasies about making off with one of the brown hessian sacks and eating rice until I burst.

I was now old enough to harvest rice, gathering the stalks in one hand and cutting them with a sickle held in the other. A sickle is a hand tool with a wickedly sharp blade that curves around until it forms three quarters of a circle. The stalks of the crop are hooked by the blade which is then drawn back to complete the cut. It paid to keep your wits about you while learning to use this implement and I thought I was getting the hang of it until I cut my little finger to the bone. I stifled a cry of pain and examined the bleeding finger. I wanted to cry but I was afraid of the Khmer Rouge brigade leaders. I never knew what they might do to me if I drew their attention in any way, but I did know that I must work in order to avoid punishment. I had heard somewhere that spider silk would stop bleeding, so I found a cobweb amongst the rice plants and used it as a bandage. It did stop the blood flowing but my finger still became infected and flared with pain every time I bumped it for weeks afterwards. I learned my lesson and was more careful after that.

Again that harvest year, we had to work through most of the night under the reluctant light of the oil lamps, beating the rice from the stalks. This was after a full day bent over, cutting the rice and bundling it into sheaves ready to be carried back to the central processing area. I was so tired and felt so sleepy that I took a risk and rested behind the haystack, for what was meant to be just a moment. I promptly fell asleep unnoticed by the others, who continued to throw the discarded hay onto the pile. I quickly became completely covered and woke up early the next morning with no one around. I tiptoed into the sleeping quarters so as not to disturb the others, but more importantly I managed to avoid the notice and punishment of the Khmer Rouge guards. I shuddered to think of the example they would have made of someone who had slept while the others had worked.

The next day I woke with a fever and found that a fat tick had attached itself behind my right ear. That might have explained my tiredness from the day before and I knew that I had to get rid of it. I pulled on it but only the bottom half came out and the head remained deep inside my skin. I gritted my teeth as one of the other girls dug it out, with a sharp piece of metal that we sterilised in a fire as best we could. I did not dare cry out as the pain flared across my skin. I was afraid that the guards would hear.

During the monsoon, the humidity made it almost impossible to dry clothes. I had to try to sleep, cold and hungry in my wet uniform. Each time the threadbare cloth tore from age or the constant damp, I borrowed a needle and thread and patched it up as best I could. My once black uniforms had now faded to a light brown from constant exposure to the sun. They were worn to such tatters that I could hardly see the original material. So many patches were holding them together, haphazardly sewn one on top of the next, that the garments became thick and bulky.

Every night for four years, I lay on the bare earth, exhausted, dirty and hungry. Every night for four years, I cried because I missed my family. Every night for four years, I went to sleep terrified that this would be the night I would be dragged from my squalid bed at the whim of the brigade leader, to be tortured, raped or killed. No one cared. We were all having the same nightmares.

My time in the child labour brigade was the worst time of my life, but I survived where uncounted thousands did not. While I was engaged in my own struggles, my sisters and brothers were trapped in similar situations. My older sister Bouy was spending her days carrying soil from place to place for *Angkar*'s endless and largely pointless construction projects. Keang and Houy were with her in the same camp, keeping their heads down like the rest of us. Bouy's only tools for the task of carting dirt were a pair of woven baskets and a pole made by splitting a length of bamboo down the middle. The baskets were suspended at each end of the pole, which was held across her aching shoulders. To ensure that the teenagers in her brigade did not slack off they were not permitted to load their own baskets. The brigade leaders always made sure that they were full to the brim.

One day Bouy was given a load of wet and heavy soil and the pole she was using snapped under the strain. Bamboo was the most common construction material in Cambodia because of its strength and plentiful supply. Some species of bamboo replaced themselves so fast that Bouy's pole represented about a week's growth. It was not something to get upset about, not unless you were a mindless servant of *Angkar* and intent on finding fault whether it made sense or not.

Bouy was singled out as being wasteful, of being *kmang*—the enemy—for destroying *Angkar*'s property. She was thrust into the centre of the circle during the endless nightly meetings and condemned for her actions every night. Other workers fell prey to this attitude, glad that they were at least out of the firing line for a while. They harassed her about the incident, lest they were noticed by the leaders for not joining in. Bouy found it hard to cope with the guilt and could only take so much. She feared that *Angkar* would persecute the rest of us as well, since we were the family of the enemy. We had survived this far by escaping notice, working hard and doing what we were told. If we were examined closely by the brigade leaders they would discover our Chinese blood. We would surely be sent to the mass graves along with so many others.

My three sisters and a few other girls went to a nearby well to wash themselves, under the shade of a big *Kor* tree. When they were ready to head back to camp, Bouy told them to go on ahead without her, saying that she would take a moment to wash her clothes and would catch up with them soon. Bouy did not return to the sleeping quarters that night and the next morning her sisters returned to the well to find her. They searched the area and called her name but there was no response. Finally they looked up.

Bouy had hung herself with her red scarf, the symbol of *Angkar's* paradise. The brigade leader arrived on the scene and ordered Keang and Houy back to work, before climbing into the tree to cut through the branch, sending Bouy's body thudding to the earth.

Bouy is buried under a tree somewhere in Cambodia. A shallow grave was dug and she joined so many others under the killing fields. We were never told where she was buried. There was no one there to mourn my sister. She was seventeen.

Mother and the Tiger

In 1979 I was twelve years old and my brigade was in the cassava fields clearing weeds. We had been working for hours and looking forward to the midday break where we could sit for a while and eat our one meal for the day. Since dawn there had been odd noises in the distance, thuds that sounded like the explosions we remembered from the time of the Vietnam War, but artillery or air strikes could not be the source. There was no one who could challenge *Angkar*. Surely the world had abandoned Cambodia as effectively as any country in history.

As usual, I had my head down and was working as hard as I could to avoid the wrath of the brigade leaders. Eventually I glanced around and noticed that none of the Khmer Rouge brigade leaders were watching us. In fact, there was no sign of them anywhere at all. This was unprecedented in the four years they had been in control. The other children had noticed this absence as well, and were looking at each other with expressions on their faces that plainly asked: 'What now?'

For a while we were frozen with indecision, thinking that this must surely be a trap and that if we left our assignments we would be punished. One of those ragged, skinny little girls came to a decision. She took a few hesitant steps and then halted. No one appeared out of the undergrowth to stop her. No reprimand or punishment seemed imminent. After a few seconds she dropped the hoe she had been using and just ran.

We followed her. Every last one of us followed her. The Khmer Rouge was gone.

The arrival of *yuon*, the Vietnamese army, into Cambodia caused utter pandemonium, a chaos so complete that it made the original exodus from the cities seem mild in comparison. Faced with the advancing troops, the Khmer Rouge melted into the jungle without a word to their victims. We were meant to be under their care so that a new and pure society could be created. The way they abandoned their posts was just a parting reminder of the contempt that they had always held for us. Although they no longer controlled Cambodia, the dying spasms of the regime continued to warp my country for decades to come. One aspect of *Angkar* that disintegrated the moment the guards left was the forced marriages of the people who had originally come from the cities. There had been few new children born over the previous four years and they stayed with their mothers. In stark contrast, the original village dwellers often stayed with the partners the Khmer Rouge had chosen for them.

I did not pause to think about the situation, I just wanted to get as far away as I could, as fast as possible. I ran to the hut where we had slept and gathered my few belongings. I wrapped them in my red scarf, swung the bundle over my shoulder and followed a crowd that increased in size by the minute. People appeared out of the jungle from wherever they had been working, no longer separated by age and sex. The gathering tide of humanity did not know what was happening or what the future held, but no one wanted to stay where they were for one more minute. Every camp was abandoned. The empty woven baskets that had been used just minutes before for hauling dirt were scattered on the ground.

Everyone was free to go where they pleased, but virtually everyone in my area went the same way. Initially we headed in whatever direction took us out of the jungle as quickly as possible. Then we all turned east, a river of people flowing along the dusty road, walking barefoot on their callused feet. We were all driven by the same demons and the same urge to get far away from the horror that had befallen us. Our bodies were weak with starvation and disease, but nothing short of death could have kept us in a place with so many terrible memories. Everyone ran to try to reunite themselves with their families, but many would never find their loved ones. Almost a quarter of the country's population had perished under *Angkar's* rule, and few families were left untouched.

The Khmer Rouge had never used motorised transport to move people around. Instead they marched their captives from place to place, at the point of a gun if necessary. Families had been torn apart and their members sent to different camps. Mostly though, they had always been within walking distance of each other if they only knew the direction to go. They had no idea where their sons and daughters were, but most people were following a similar path and families began to reunite as people found each other amidst the throng. People were running around like headless chickens and there was panic everywhere. Children were crying and adults were shouting to each other, as they spied loved ones that they had not seen in four years.

I was more alone than I had ever been in my life. Before the Khmer Rouge I had always had my parents and brothers and sisters. Then *Angkar* had become a surrogate parent, though a brutal one. Now I was surrounded by people who were searching for their own families. They had no time to help me and there were no authorities to care for one scared child. There was certainly no help for the thousands of children wandering aimlessly through the crowd, hoping to catch sight of parents who may no longer have been alive.

I was only twelve years old and like the other lost children I did not know where to go or what to do. I did not know the way back to the village where my family had originally been together, so I simply followed the crowd east, hoping to find someone. *Anyone.* After several hours I arrived at a junction. The path I had been on crossed the main road where another, even bigger crowd was snaking past heading south. An endless line of people marched on the road, some clutching babies in their arms. Some carried pots and pans or other items they had liberated as they fled their work camps. Some carried bundles of looted possessions on their heads. Some had nothing more than the clothes they were wearing.

Young children were tugged along, their hands gripped tightly by their mothers or older siblings. I looked at them and wished I was holding my mother's hand. I had spent four years surviving on nothing but my wits and a healthy dose of luck that seemed well overdue to run out. I wanted to be cared for by my parents again. Now that the nightmare of the Khmer Rouge was fading, it was being replaced by another: one where I wandered alone amongst the indifferent crowd and died beside the road.

I was frantic to search for my family but at the same time was wracked with indecision. Should I wait and hope that I could catch sight of them as they passed? But what if they had already gone by? I might never catch up if I waited too long. In the end, I was frozen by my fears and just waited on the roadside, my eyes flicking from one face to the next, desperately hoping to find just one that was familiar to me. I tried not to think about the possibility that I would never see any of them again. I tried not to imagine that they were all dead.

I stood there for hours watching people go past, sometimes crying in misery and sometimes shouting in a vain attempt to be heard over the uproar. My voice was utterly lost amidst so many others, but no matter how hopeless I felt I endlessly scanned the crowd. I constantly saw what I thought were members of my family and threw myself in their direction, only to discover that I was mistaken. Every time I would return to my lookout and resume my search. By the late afternoon I had begun to panic in earnest, but still I could not tear myself away from my vantage point. Never in my life had I been unsupervised after dark and I knew that night would soon fall. I had not eaten anything since the day before, and little enough then. I had been scared the whole day thinking that my family had already gone on ahead. Now that it was getting dark a new terror grew in me. I had not seen any of them for so long that maybe I had simply not recognised them, and they had walked right by me.

Finally, just as the sun was setting, I saw a familiar face in the crowd for what seemed the hundredth time that day. It did not matter how many times I had been wrong before, I shoved my way into the mass of people, shouting out to her. I ran the last few metres hoping that finally, after four years of unbroken nightmare, I would at last be with my family again. This time I was not disappointed. I ran into my mother's embrace.

I was utterly ecstatic, but as I hugged her I also saw Khay, Mei, Veng and finally Father. It turned out that they had all been to the north of the crossroads and were now going south. They had not expected to find me at all. Our meeting was nothing more than lucky timing and if I had delayed arriving at the crossroads for a single day then I would probably never have seen any of them again. Mother told me that Houy had been with them up until a few hours before, but she had become separated from them among the crowd. They had no idea where my older siblings Keang and Huor were, or even if they were still alive.

It was bad enough that she had lost her daughter so soon after being reunited, but to make matters worse, Houy had been carrying all the gold that Mother had kept hidden so carefully for so long. With Houy being the oldest child present, my parents had used material to strap the gold around her waist. The metal was the closest thing Cambodia had to a currency at that time, and we would desperately need it in the weeks to come. We thought that she must have gone on ahead because my father could only move slowly and Houy had been strong. There was nothing to do but continue to move away from the hated camps and hope that we would catch up to Houy, or that she would somehow find us. We would go south at dawn.

In the light of the new day I got my first good look at my family. We were all burned a deep brown by our years in the sun. This went against traditional ideas of beauty, but in truth it had been good camouflage and had probably saved our lives when pale Chinese were being hunted by the Khmer Rouge. My parents seemed to have aged twenty years, though we had only been parted for four. Their eyes were sunken, their arms and legs were like brittle sticks and their skin was thin and fragile. We children were shadows of our former selves but even after all I had witnessed, the sight of Mei horrified me. Veng woke up and took one look at his twin before yelling, 'Mum, Mei is a ghost!' He had good reason; my sister looked like a skeleton that had wrapped itself in an ill-fitting skin it had found somewhere. She could not walk, she could not even talk, only nodding or shaking her head in answer to Mother's many questions. She later told me that she had been afraid that if she opened her mouth the last of her strength would slip away and she would die right then and there. Mother had to carry Mei in her arms.

When the guards had disappeared into the jungle, Mei had gone to Veng's camp and the pair of them had made their way back to the village where my father had been living the entire time. They knew the way well because, as it turned out, the pair of them had frequently run away. Each time they did, their guards would come looking for them and drag them back to the work camps. Mei had once hidden by rolling herself in a sleeping mat and lying still, while the hut was searched by the increasingly exasperated Khmer Rouge soldier sent to find her. My father was afraid that the enraged guard would decide to make an example of her or kill her outright, and pointed out her hiding place. Mei had been furious with him, but she survived the experience.

Along with a group of other survivors, we made our way along the Mekong River. Whenever we saw an abandoned warehouse along the way, we would take as much food as we could carry. We felt no guilt at raiding the buildings after slaving to grow so much food and receiving very little in return. We kept moving because of the sounds of conflict in the distance. Occasionally there were the dull hollow explosions of artillery, and constantly the quick popping reports of rifles. The Vietnamese army was harrying the Khmer Rouge, which was fine by us but we did not want to become caught up in the fighting. When two armies clash in civilian populated areas, the non-combatants usually end up contributing most to the body count. I could not stand the idea that after surviving so much I might be killed by a random bullet. There was no particular fear though; that emotion had been burned away until the struggle to stay alive was all that was left.

Angkar could never win. Their ragtag soldiers were very effective in terrorising unarmed civilians, but they were no match for the properly trained and equipped Vietnamese army. Whenever the Khmer Rouge dug in they were targeted by mortars or artillery and forced to run for their worthless lives. I had hoped that they were scared before they died.

It seemed as if the whole world was on the move. Thousands of people carried their few belongings in baskets and bundles tied to both ends of a long stick and balanced on their shoulders. Everyone was walking and sometimes running away from the areas under fire, away from the chaos. We would walk as far as we could before stopping to rest. This was not far because my father was old and had not been treated well in the camps. He was very weak but we followed the crowd as best we could.

My youngest brother Veng was only capable of carrying a light burden, so he was given a kettle to lug along. Father could not walk unassisted and neither could Mei, who was also very weak. Mother, Khay and I carried the rest of the family's belongings, which mostly consisted of whatever food we had been able to find. I watched in weary disbelief as Mother walked three times as fast as the rest of us, with a stick on her shoulders and bundles of possessions tied to either end. She would walk fifty metres ahead, set down her burden and then return to pick up Mei in her arms and carry her to the bundle of goods. Mother walked triple the distance of the rest of my family, hour after hour, all day and every day, for more than a week.

As we walked we constantly saw the results of the Khmer Rouge's insanity. There were dead bodies everywhere and Veng became very distressed at the sight of them. He began to scream and cry uncontrollably, before finally subsiding into an exhausted whimpering. Some of the bodies had lain there for years, and some had died during our exodus as their bodies finally failed them. Some had fallen victim to the ongoing fighting after surviving the worst humanity had to offer. We could not attempt to bury them. We had neither the time nor the strength, and sometimes there were so many that we had to step over them to continue on our journey. In the heat the bodies of those killed in the fighting swelled up and began to rot. The stench of death lingered over the road like an invisible fog that I thought I could never leave behind. The corpses were covered with frenzied flies and were full of maggots. At times we came across older sites where hundreds of people had been rounded up and slaughtered in the early days of *Angkar*. It was horrifying to walk through the sun bleached skeletal remains, but at least these old atrocities had lost the worst of their smell.

Thankfully it was the dry season, because we had no shelter whatsoever. Dry was a relative term in Cambodia though, and even without the monsoon there was always plenty of water to drink. We knew we would have to cross the Mekong River; it was the only way to get away from the constant bombing and rifle fire being exchanged between the Vietnamese army and the remnants of the Khmer Rouge. When we came to the mighty river we slept on its bank the first night. We had to cross the huge stretch of water, but that was a problem that would have to wait until morning.

During the dry season, sections of the river were dotted with sand bars and the water was mostly shallow enough to wade through. After travelling south for several hours, we found a wide and shallow part of the stream where we could wade across. This was fortunate because none of us could swim very well at all. The Mekong was kilometres wide in the places where it ran shallow, and we had to zigzag back and forth to stay on the sand banks and avoid the deeper water. It took us hours to cross, and all the while bloated bodies of animals, men, women and children constantly drifted by at the same slow, stately speed. I dreaded the touch of the river, thinking that it must consist more of blood than water. In the wet season the Mekong swelled, and if we had been travelling at that time it would have been impossible to cross. We would have been trapped between the waters and the conflict that was constantly threatening to overtake us.

After crossing the river we found a road that went south and kept going. We had to keep moving if we wanted any hope of finding safety and a chance to put our shattered lives back together. We were crusted with mud from head to toe, and exhausted from carrying heavy loads for long hours. All along the road thousands upon thousands of people camped each night, cooking whatever meagre supplies of food they had been able to find along the way. They kept their belongings close because there was no law; possession was everything. All we had to cook with was the kettle that Veng carried each day. Our only food was the dried rice that Mother had saved when she worked as a chef in the camps. We would fill the kettle with water, bring it to boil, then pour in some rice and let it stand to soften. Eating the rice was awkward at best, but it was all that we possessed and it was more than many other families had.

After travelling south for several days we struck up a conversation with another family who were able to move more quickly than us. They had followed the same route away from the fighting and had seen my sister Houy. They told us that she was some way behind, but at least heading south like us. Khay and I decided that we could not wait for our lost big sister to catch up. Instead we set off running back up the road to find her. Our family could get some badly needed rest until we returned. We had not run very far before our lack of food forced us to slow down to a walk. On the way north we passed the place where we had crossed the Mekong, but decided to keep going. If Houy had crossed there then she would find the rest of our family, and if she had crossed further to the north then we would find her.

Khay and I had set off in such a rush that we had not brought any food with us, not that there was much that we could have taken. Because we were further north than where most people crossed the river, we found some trees with ripe fruit that had not been stripped bare by other travellers. The fruit was called *kwart* and was traditionally eaten under-ripe, when the inside was powdery, dry and rather bitter. These were ripe though, the way I had always preferred, when the flesh had become sticky and sweet like tamarind. Opening the fruit was usually accomplished with an axe because the outer skin was incredibly hard. We had no tools and had to make do with a rock. We stuffed ourselves until we thought we would burst and wrapped as much as we could carry in our red scarves. We had not abandoned the scarves, though they reminded us every minute of the hell we had been through. We had so few belongings that nothing could go to waste. The *kwart* was the best meal that I had eaten since Father had cooked me some rice with pork fat, almost four years before. We swung the heavy bundles over our shoulders and kept going.

As we walked we were given strange looks by the masses of people going in the opposite direction. No one in their right mind should have been going north at all, let alone two determined looking children with a sense of mission about them. Mad, they obviously thought, completely mad. To the north was conflict, bombs and death. I was with Khay though, and that meant that everything would be fine. Once we were north of our earlier river crossing, the crowds decreased until the number of people we saw dropped to almost nothing. This did not last though. The Khmer Rouge had been driven out of the country to the west of the Mekong later than the areas to the east, where my family had been. Now those recently freed people reached us and we had to begin scanning hundreds of faces for a glimpse of our sister.

We passed through the sea of unfamiliar people. They all had the same haunted eyes. They had all seen and experienced too much. They were all running away from the memories that they had been accumulating until just a few days before. Everybody was dressed in the black pyjama-like uniforms that the Khmer Rouge had forced upon us and we had come to resemble the Western stereotype. We did indeed all look very much the same. The task seemed hopeless, but Khay's natural determination was unshaken by his miserable time in the camps, and he refused to admit to failure. We would return with our sister or not at all. I had no complaints because I knew that if I was ever lost then Khay would find me, no matter what. The afternoon began to turn to dusk and I became worried that we would not find Houy before nightfall. It felt like a repeat of the day I stood and waited at the crossroads, hoping to catch sight of anyone from my family.

As the sun touched the horizon we finally spotted a face that we knew. We ran forward in joy as we found our sister at last and wrapped her in a rib crushing hug. At that moment anything seemed possible as long as I had Khay leading the way. Surely my big sister Keang and big brother Huor would also soon be found. They did not show any signs of emerging from the crowd that very minute though, and so we turned around and retraced our steps to the south.

As we travelled back towards the rest of our family we shared our hoard of fruit with Houy. We ate as much as we could when we got back to the trees and then picked more to take back to our parents. The nightmare of *Angkar* might have been over but we knew we had to take every opportunity to feed ourselves. As we walked day turned into night, and when it was completely dark we still had a long way to go. We did not want to stop at night and risk losing contact with everyone else if they were forced to move early in the morning, so we kept going. With Khay leading us we were not afraid of the night, and he was determined to reunite as much of his family as he could. Sometime that night we reached our parents and dropped to the ground beside them, exhausted but thoroughly happy for the first time that we could remember.

Now that Houy was back with us, she could ease Mother's burden and we could increase our pace in our journey south. Now Mother only had to carry Mei and did not have to double back every few minutes, but it would take another two weeks for Mei to recover enough to walk on her own. For that entire time my mother carried her daughter without complaint. We travelled with a large group of people feeling like there was a sense of safety in numbers. Our problem was that we could not possibly move as fast as everyone else. Not only was Mother carrying Mei, but Father was only capable of a painfully slow shuffle, and he could carry nothing. We children had to carry most of our possessions, and we were all weighed down to our limits. Each evening we would catch up to the main body of refugees who had already set up camp. We would see the spires of their campfires rising into the sky for an hour or more before we arrived and could finally rest for the night. After we staggered into the camp we would find that hundreds of people had long since taken the best sites. If we did not manage to catch up by nightfall then we slept alongside the road and left early the next day to catch up.

The fruit that we had found did not last long and our diet consisted almost entirely of rice with a little salt. We rarely managed to acquire any meat but I noticed that some other families seemed to have plenty. During the dispersal of people from the camps, even animals had sensed the urgency to escape and had scattered in all directions. Some people had taken carts and oxen when they had fled and as a result they could ride all day rather than walk. They had the energy to catch the loose domestic animals, and the means to carry them. It hardly seemed fair to me, but the concept of fair no longer held sway in my world.

The strain of constant travel combined with his age brought my father to a standstill. He was sixty-eight years old by then and could no longer walk, even with the aid of his stick. Mother hired a seat for Father on an ox cart with some of her dwindling supply of gold. Ever since our reunion I had seen other families with their strong fathers carrying most of their belongings and doing most of the work. I looked at my family and saw that my father was too old to walk, let alone carry anything. I resented Mother for marrying him and I resented Father for being too old to be helpful. Ever since we had been forced out of Kratie, Father had taken a minor role in the family dynamic. Khay was not the oldest child at just fourteen years of age, but he knew that someone had to take charge. He stepped up as the male head of the family and none of us objected. He seemed to know what he was doing.

I made a promise to myself that if I was ever to marry I would not choose an older man like Mother had. I was too young to consider that without the blight of the Khmer Rouge, my mother's choice would have been sound. She could not have known what was going to befall us, and neither could Father. None of my family deserved the slightest blame and the collective misery endured by every man, woman and child in Cambodia should have been laid across the backs of the Khmer Rouge leaders until their spines snapped like rotten twigs. That their names would become curses to rival that of Stalin or Hitler was of little solace. I was too young and I blamed those closest to me.

Everyone on the road south was travelling as fast as they could. We were pursued by the constant fighting and no one had the time, energy or inclination to bury bodies. The sheer number of dead people scattered across the countryside was the ultimate testament to the insanity that had overtaken Cambodia. We had been walking for days, and still we passed hundreds of bloated dead bodies, left on the side of the road like so much unwanted trash. The sky was our roof now and the dirt was our bed. The moon and the stars had replaced the electric lights we once had. Our routine was simple; we walked most of the day and slept during the night. There was nothing else to do apart from keep constant watch for food and any signs of danger.

We journeyed through many villages and always searched them for anything useful. We were rarely the first on the scene and so anything valuable for survival had already been raided. We scrounged around for food and searched for any practical items anyway. There was nothing else to do and any possibility was worth a look. We rested in each village we encountered, with no complaint from the prior residents, who had already fled or been killed. Explosions sounded in the distance. Sometimes they sounded closer, causing people to look over their shoulders nervously and quicken their pace. The airplanes from the Vietnamese forces roared overhead, bound with deadly intent for pockets of resistance. Smoke billowed into the sky behind us, sometimes lit from beneath by sudden bursts of bright light, but always glowing with the blood red taint of the flames.

Most of the time there was no village to rest in, or if there was it was already full by the time we arrived. On one occasion we stopped for the night in a plantation of rubber trees. The ground under the trees was thickly carpeted with leaves and we piled them up to use as bedding. We were told not to start any fires because of the flammable leaves, and it was thought that the trees would burn quickly if set alight. Khay and I went in search of water and wandered down a slope where we found a running creek. It was lucky that we found a source of water because without a fire we could not cook our rice. We did not have anything to eat that night at all and drank lots of water to fill our growling bellies. At night we crowded together as the mosquitoes feasted on our blood and large red ants bit our legs. In the morning I had red welts on my hands and legs that itched unbearably. We endured the insects and hoped that nothing larger and hungrier would come calling. Because we were always on the edge of camp we were vulnerable to wild animals, animals that preferred fresh meat and stalked through the jungle's shadows. The most dangerous of these was the Asian tiger, a predator that was known to be a man-eater.

We arrived at a campsite behind everyone else as usual, hungry and totally exhausted. My body ached with pain from walking so far, but I helped to arrange our few possessions on the very edge of the jungle. The trees were a menacing presence that I never became used to. I thought I should be immune by now to the dense growth and the terrors that dwelled just out of sight. As the fear of the Khmer Rouge had faded, my fear of insects getting into my ears had resurfaced. Fatigue overcame fear though, and after I lay down I fell straight to sleep on the hard ground. Mother did not sleep much, instead keeping watch over her family. She lit a small fire to protect us from dangerous animals. After losing and surviving so much I thought that she was determined to preserve what she had left. Every now and then I would wake and see her sitting motionless but awake and watchful for danger. Reassured, I would fall back to sleep and leave the worrying to her.

In the dead of night I was shaken awake and sat up, still half asleep. A hissed warning from Mother brought me fully alert and she pointed towards the trees. My heart skipped a beat. In the flickering light of the fire I could see two huge luminous eyes staring back at me. A tiger, 180 kilograms of toothed and clawed death. In that moment it did not matter that compared to the Khmer Rouge, tigers hardly ever hurt anyone at all. This cat was three metres from nose to tail and *right there*! Mother slowly picked up some sticks and laid them in the fire, never looking away from the tiger's eyes for an instant.

The flames began to burn higher and in the brighter light we could see the tiger stalking out of the jungle towards us. I was terrified and started drawing breath to scream and wake the rest of my family. I turned in time to see Mother advancing on the huge predator. She was a quarter its size and had spent the last four years on a starvation diet. That tiger was well fed, strong, and had spent its life hunting far bigger and better armed prey. Mother brandished a flaming tree branch in either hand and cursed the animal with words that I had never heard before.

The tiger snarled and crouched as it prepared to attack. Time seemed to slow to a crawl as Mother swung the flaring wood past the animal's nose and then hurled one of the branches into its face. The tiger hissed at her and paused to consider its position; this small, loud, spitting woman was plainly trouble. It backed up a step, then turned around and silently retreated into the jungle. The tiger paused once and glanced over its shoulder at us. I think it wanted to make sure that my mother was not coming after it.

- 13 -

Irony

We had been travelling along the Mekong for three weeks, following the river as it curved west and then back to the south. We seemed to have left the worst of the fighting behind us, although we still heard the distant sounds of artillery from time to time. We were almost to Kampong Cham province and more than halfway to the capital of Phnom Penh from where we had started. Then we received some important news from the refugees that we were camped with, several of whom had managed to find small radios. They followed the progress of the Vietnamese liberation and spread the word as to what was happening in other parts of the country. A new interim government seemed to have been set up and was advising people what to do in the chaos that had followed the Khmer Rouge's overthrow.

According to the people who had heard the announcement, the soldiers of *Angkar* had been driven south-west, high into the Cardamom Mountains. Their leadership had gone into hiding and would trouble us no more. We were free to return to our homes or to go anywhere else we chose. The large group we had been travelling with rapidly broke up as people headed for their former homes or in whatever direction seemed to offer the best prospects. Mother thought that we should stick to the direction we had been going. We were already most of the way to Kampong Cham where her family had lived. At least some of them should still be in the area and if so, they would have begun to re-establish themselves. With luck they would be able to help their destitute relatives.

Father would hear none of it. He decided that we would return to Kratie where our house was waiting, and we could continue with our lives that had been so abruptly disrupted six years before. Frail as he was, he remained the head of our family and would brook no dissension. It felt particularly hard because we would be going back over old ground, and there was no longer the urgency of a war at our backs. We turned around and began to retrace our steps.

It took another three unpleasant but uneventful weeks to get back to Kratie. We saw elements of the Vietnamese army on the way, as their tanks and trucks drove west to pursue the fleeing Khmer Rouge. The Vietnamese soldiers were friendly and sympathetic, but beyond that they had nothing to give us. There were millions of Cambodians in need and even if they had given us all their food they could only help a tiny percentage of the desperate population. We had survived this far on our own and would have to continue to do so. We were happy that the men with guns were only interested in shooting at *Angkar's* soldiers and not us.

We managed to get a boat ride across the Mekong, which saved us days of travel north to the point we had crossed earlier. Kratie was in sight and our journey finally seemed to be at an end. The Khmer Rouge had not bothered to raze cities to the ground and had only emptied them of their people. The town was largely intact, though there were many buildings destroyed by the events of the last four years. We held our breath as our house came into view. To our elation it was still standing and undamaged; however, all was not right. There were armed Vietnamese soldiers standing guard at the front of the house, and as we got closer they held up their hands to prevent us from entering. They were polite but nevertheless informed us that our home was now being used to house the troops and store their supplies. We tried to argue but we had no proof that the house was ours and eventually it became clear that they would not budge. I was furious that our house had been taken from us. It seemed as though the world was determined to strip us of everything and there was nothing I could do about it. Father realised that just like the night when Keang had burned his money, there was nothing to be done. He turned his back on the house he had worked so hard to build for his family and walked away. Only those people attached to some part of the new administration or members of the army were allowed to live in the city. So we made our way to the edge of town and set up camp as best we could.

It was not the last that Father heard on the matter. Mother complained that he should have followed her advice in the first place and that our journey had been a waste of time. She said that we should have stayed in Kampong Cham with her family. She may have been right, but there was no way to know that at the time and what else could Father have done? He was simply trying to set things back to where they had been before *Angkar*, and we could hardly blame him for that. The weeks we had spent travelling had made tempers short, and they were not helped by the realisation that once again we had nowhere to go.

There were people who had made it to Kratie and were in terrible physical condition. They had been in jail or re-education camps from which no one was meant to escape with their life. They had been fed virtually nothing and worked almost to death. Faced with such an influx of desperately hungry people, the newly formed local administration and Vietnamese army did what they could to make food available to the arrivals. They were well meaning, but without the proper advice they did not know that they were making a mistake. The wretched, skeletal men and women slumped onto the ground with bowls full of rice. They had eaten almost nothing for as long as they could remember, and suddenly they were given all they wanted. They crammed themselves with as much rice as their shrunken stomachs could hold. It was too much.

My family and I had stuffed ourselves until we were fit to burst and suffered no ill effects, but others were not so lucky. There is a condition that I later learned is called 're-feeding syndrome'. As the name suggests, it happens when a starvation victim eats too much, too quickly. The people finished their meals and then sat quietly for a while, perhaps unable to believe that their long nightmare was over. Eventually they got to their feet and some fainted right then and there. Some would succumb during the next few days, with the victims failing to wake in the morning and others collapsing to the ground at random. Many of them never woke again, their bodies unable to cope with the sudden intake of food. After four years of the worst treatment that the Khmer Rouge could dispense, it was a good meal that finally killed them. The Universe seemed to have a particularly cold sense of humour.

After several days we heard that there would be a distribution of rice from the warehouses in the city. No one knew how long the mass meals would last and trust was very scarce. There were thousands of families in the area who had been forced into virtual slave labour and starved half to death in the last four years. Many parents had children whose stick-like arms and protruding bellies increased the pressure to find a reliable supply of food. In short, the chance for such desperately needed supplies could have been a recipe for a riot. The authorities had thought of this fortunately, and devised an orderly method. They made an appointment with each family, giving them a general time to come to receive their rice and making it very clear that early arrivals would go to the bottom of the list. This might not have worked except for the fact that the people had been thoroughly cowed by their recent history. For a while at least, most people followed instructions.

We went at the appointed time and waited with a dozen or so other families to receive our rice. The unprocessed grain was distributed according to the number of people in the family and it was a huge relief to actually be given a substantial amount of food. The rice we carried was all we would receive and we would have to make it last, but at least it was ours. We would have to husk and mill the rice ourselves at the communal facilities, but we all knew how to operate the machinery very well by then.

We were told that the rice we had been given was a one-off occurrence and would not happen again. It would not last until the next harvest but we did not care. We treated ourselves and I got to eat as much rice as I could. We had been gathering as much food as possible, while travelling first south and then north. This amounted to more than we had ever received or found during our time under the control of the Khmer Rouge. Rice is the staple of Cambodia, and now we had it. We did not know what was going to happen the next day; the Khmer Rouge could return or something worse could be on its way. No thought was given to tomorrow, so we ate what we wanted before anyone could take it away from us. Meals were eaten in silence and there was a constant uneasy competition to make sure that we received our share. We were unable to shake the feeling that the little we had could be taken from us in an instant. We had lost everything once and it would take a long time before we believed that there would be a future to worry about.

As we reached the outskirts of the town, Khay spotted two familiar figures on the side of the road. He let out a shout of joy as he ran to our sister Keang and brother Huor. Just like that, the last of our family's lost children were found. In the excited questioning that followed we learned that after leaving her work camp, Keang had followed the flow of most people going east. Huor had been in jail and upon his release, he too had gone east. They had met on the road but unlike me, had not found the rest of our family. Not having anywhere else to go, they headed towards Kratie in the hope that some of us had survived and done the same. If we had decided to go on to Kampong Cham, we would never have found them.

Huor and Keang had travelled to town with another family. They had not been any extra burden since none of them had any supplies to speak of, and so nothing to share. They had received their portion of rice together with the other family, but now that they were back with us their travelling companions had no intention of releasing their share of the precious food. It was not really fair, but my parents counted themselves lucky that they had found their children when others had not. We had our original portion of rice and after so much conflict we were in no mood for a fight, so we returned to our camp.

The return of our oldest siblings was a surprise but Huor in particular seemed to have led a charmed existence, albeit a rather backhanded one. He had spent three years in jail, which was not in any way a pleasant experience. The fact that he had survived defied belief. Huor had been at the mercy of a regime that was equal in brutality to any that had ever existed. He had an ethnicity that was hated by Cambodia's new leaders and he was the child of a business man. He had always liked to read and educate himself and he had been accused of laziness by leaders who valued only a person's capacity for manual labour. Whether the charges were true or not, he was in prison and presumed guilty. In short he had been a walking dead man, but here he was.

Huor's captives were no more than boys who had little else to do but mistreat their captives and make sure that they did not escape. Dispensing torture and beatings lost its appeal after a while, and Huor had always been good at telling stories. He could also play the guitar and somehow one was found within the schoolhouse turned prison, even though the leadership frowned upon such irrelevancies. Simply put, with no television, books, papers or radio, Huor was the most entertaining show around. As long as he could remember songs and old tales or make up new ones, then he stayed alive. Periodically there were public executions of prisoners by way of example to the other prisoners, and to keep the workers outside from daring to cause trouble. Whenever this happened, Huor was mysteriously overlooked and lived for another day. New guards replaced the old, but somehow Huor managed to string out his audience for almost a thousand days.

Favoured he might have been, but Huor emerged from jail a shadow of his former self. The workers in the fields had existed on less than a starvation diet but at least they could scrounge for insects, fruit and vegetables. Prisoners received even less food and had no chance to forage for anything extra, unless they could snatch a passing cockroach or rat. When we found Huor, he looked close to death. His arms and legs were just bones and his ribs were protruding from his flanks. His hair was falling out like a victim of cancer, with only a few wispy remnants clinging to his scalp as tenaciously as he had clung to life. Mother said that cats wished they had that many lives.

Father had been a businessman, Mother had held contraband and stolen food, Mei and Veng had continually run away, and Khay had always been too smart for his own good. Any of these facts could have been the death of one or all of us. Add the target that our Chinese origins painted on every member of my family, and people thought it a miracle that so many of us had survived.

Only my big sister Bouy had not made it to the reunion. She had worked hard every day and had never made any trouble or hurt anyone. She tried to meet the demands of her captors no matter how unreasonable they were. She kept her head down and just tried to survive in the same way I had, but a stupid stick had led directly to her death. Our survival was not so much a miracle then, and those that lived or died had their fates decided by dumb luck. I no longer believed in miracles, where the lucky and the prosperous congratulated themselves on the intervention of the spirits when they benefited from good fortune. If anyone had deserved such help, it had been Bouy.

My parents held firmly to their Buddhist beliefs and believed in *kam*, that acts committed in the present life will affect future life. They said that it was their many generous donations to the *wat* before the Khmer Rouge regime that had built up their Karma. It came back to repay them and had saved our lives. The manner of a person's death did not matter, just how they lived their life. Presumably Bouy would be rewarded in her next incarnation, since there could be none in this one. I was doubtful, but I did not contradict them.

After about a week in Kratie it was clear to my parents that nothing was going to change with regard to our house. Each family was now responsible for its own affairs. It was unlikely that there would be any more food distributions and we needed to find somewhere to live. We left town on foot and went to a village about fifteen kilometres east of the Mekong River. Leaving Kratie again felt like it did when the Khmer Rouge evacuated the city, but at least there were no soldiers pointing guns at us this time. We camped along the roadside and reached the village the next day.

Like much of Cambodia, the area around the new village was divided into the regular rice paddies that the Khmer Rouge had favoured. We had the rice that we had been given but it clearly was not going to last for long. We had only just arrived but we immediately began to supplement our supplies by scouring the rice fields, looking for rice heads that had been dropped during the harvest. It was familiar work. During our times in the work camps the children were often ordered to glean whatever rice had fallen to the ground. This time we had the incentive that we were working for our family, rather than *Angkar*. We also had Khay. Others had picked up the easily seen rice heads, but we were determined to catch up. Though it was already late in the afternoon and we had spent all day walking, we joined the others who already had nearly full bags and got to work.

We walked slowly across the field, stooping to gather any leftover heads of rice. Khay was determined that we would have our share and drove us younger children on. Everyone else had long since left before we returned to our parents with our booty. Khay roused us from our sleep and set us to work the next morning before anyone else had arrived. Actually it was before the sun had even risen. Others joined us and resumed their search in the hot sun, but with Khay instructing us we gathered more rice than anyone else there. It did not matter if we had enough for our own family; we had to have more than anyone else around. Khay had always been competitive whenever we so much as played a simple game. Now with so much hunger in his recent past and food for the taking, he was unstoppable.

- 14 -

Just Rewards

We found an abandoned stilt hut next to a large *Kor* tree and since no one objected, we moved in. We ended up sharing half of the six by four metre space with another ethnic Chinese family, who had suffered similar persecution to us under the rule of the Khmer Rouge. Between both families there were thirteen people altogether. The first time it rained it became obvious why the hut had been left empty. The thatched roof leaked so badly that it offered only slightly more protection than the tree outside. The holes in the ceiling merely served to concentrate the falling water into so many mini waterfalls that there was no space large enough for any of us to lie down at night. I would find a spot in between the cold streams that was merely damp and sit upright, dozing as best I could.

The hut was about half a metre off the ground with a two-step ladder at the doorway. It may have had a leaky roof but at least we no longer had to lie on the dirt. I was very pleased about this, for the fear of insects crawling into my ears had never once left me in the four years I had been sleeping on the ground. There was no running water in the hut, or anywhere in the village for that matter. We collected fresh water from a well in the middle of the rice paddies, although it was more of an ooze than a well. Like our hut it had been abandoned by the resident villagers, who had deeper and faster flowing wells on their own properties. It consisted of a hole about three metres deep with a lethargic trickle of water in the bottom. I had to lower myself into the well with a rope and use a bowl to scoop the water a little at a time into a bucket. It took hours to fill our two buckets, one mouthful at a time.

We did all our cooking under the big *Kor* tree that stood about five metres away from the hut. The tree had large pods with soft fluffy stuff inside that resembled cotton wool and harnessed the wind to scatter its seeds. When the pods were young the contents tasted slightly sweet, something like the silk on the top of a cob of corn, and after maturing the dry fluff could be used for stuffing pillows. At the front of the hut was the dirt road that ran through the village and behind were rice fields. We did not have any land to grow food, so we spent our days searching the nearby jungle for fruit, vegetables and mushrooms. We could once again wear coloured clothing if we had it but we were still barefooted. There were no schools in the region and our situation felt like a milder version of the Khmer Rouge regime.

Though we were free from the hateful clutches of *Angkar*, we were still in a terrible position. Aside from the earlier distribution of rice we had to fend for ourselves and once again my brother Khay took it upon himself to be the provider for the family. Although he could not tell Mother and Father what to do, he became the leader of the children. He rapidly became impatient with anyone who did not follow his instructions quickly or closely enough, and so I became his shadow. I was small, fast and willing to take orders. I admired him for his bravery and his unceasing effort in acquiring more food for our family.

One day Khay and I went to gather young bamboo shoots

from along the creek that ran through the jungle near our hut. We were ankle deep in mud and I was busy breaking off the shoots to add to our already sizable haul. I did not realise that a large and apparently starving leech had latched onto my leg. Leeches have a natural anaesthetic in their saliva that numbs their victim and prevents them from feeling the attack. The saliva also contains an anti-coagulant to keep the blood flowing freely. When we moved to another area I noticed the slimy finger sized creature and shrieked with terror. I splashed wildly through the mud, yelling for help and running out of the water. This did not bother the leech at all. I was so scared of those blood sucking parasites that I began to shake uncontrollably.

Khay was unimpressed. He told me off for being scared of the creature, saying that it could not kill me. He told me to stand still so that he could snatch it off my leg. It took several goes before he got a strong enough grip, hurling the leech into the trees when it finally came away from my skin. I did not know if he was scared of the leeches himself and had no choice but to be brave for me. Maybe he had simply had the fear burned out of him during his time in the work camps. Either way he was fearless in my eyes.

My oldest sister Keang and I went to pick green leafy water vegetables known locally as *trokuon* or wild morning glory. The plant grew all over the rice paddy and only the young shoots were edible, but there was plenty of them. Initially I was very greedy and was determined to pick every last bit to take home and show Khay. We were knee deep in water and had not been gathering the plant for long when I noticed another of the cursed leeches had attached itself to me. I lost all interest in my task and ran to stand on dry ground. I started jumping up and down, hoping that the leech would shake off or be persuaded to let go on its own. It did not and this time Khay was not around to help me. Keang was just as scared of it as I was and was no help at all. Instead I gathered a handful of grass and used it to scrape the awful thing off my leg.

Rice had become a currency in Cambodia, since there was by then no form of paper money to exchange. Useful items or precious metals were always of value but they were kept for emergencies. We had nothing else to trade, however, so Mother bartered with another villager and swapped a small amount of gold for a serviceable bicycle. There was no way her family was going to remain stuck in such a miserable situation if she had any say in the matter. She cycled to Kratie and used her gold to obtain bulk items that she could on-sell to the local villagers. She bought fishing lines, garlic, MSG flavour enhancer, fish paste in large containers, and various sizes of plastic bags. We squatted under the *Kor* tree and made up small bags of the items, sometimes as little as a teaspoon of MSG at a time. Houy and I went door to door, exchanging the items for rice until we had as much as we could carry home. Using this method, we were able to barter for triple the amount of rice that Mother's gold would have purchased on its own.

As we criss-crossed the village, we came across a big stilt house with vines in the front. The vines produced the sort of leaves Mother used when she chewed betel nut. She had not been able to find either the nuts or leaves for a long time, and I knew that she would love to get at least one of the ingredients. I tried to exchange some of our goods for the betel leaves but the owner refused. After dinner I told Khay about the vine and how much it would please Mother if we could get her some of the leaves. Khay had been out in the jungle all day gathering edible plants for dinner, but immediately hatched a plan. That night he and I did not sleep. Instead we waited until everyone else had retired to sleep and then we stole out of the hut. We walked across the village by sticking to the shadows, heading towards the house.

Everyone in the village was asleep and it was very quiet, except for the noise of insects going about their honest business, unlike us. The moon lit our way and we were able to see quite clearly in the open areas. We tiptoed under some mango trees that were so thick and dark that we could not see. With our sight removed our sense of smell was heightened, which was an unfortunate turn of events since we now found ourselves knee deep in fresh and sloppy cow dung. We stank but we had smelt far worse, and kept going. We finally reached our target undetected, where Khay instructed me to go closer to the house to keep watch and to make a secret sound if I saw the owner emerge. To do this I wormed my way through the barbed wire fence and ducked down, alert to any sound.

Khay boldly climbed the fence and proceeded to tear off every young leaf he could reach, stuffing them into his shirt as he did so. The leaves came free with a ripping sound and the vines thrashed back and forth under the sudden assault. It was at this point that we discovered that the owners of the house also owned a dog, and an aggressive one at that. The dog started to bark and then, either spotting or smelling us, charged towards me. Khay was not deaf so I forgot all about secret noises and sprinted for the fence, expecting to hear shouts and running footsteps join the dog at any instant. With my heart pounding in my chest I reached the fence and dove through the gap where I had entered.

I think most cultures probably have some form of a proverb, cautioning that 'more haste equals less speed'. In Cambodia we were told that 'he who would act quickly should learn patience'. Both are correct.

I was caught in the barbed wire like a fly in a web. Whenever I wriggled the wire only tightened its grip. I looked to where Khay was crouching in the shadows and frantically waving at me to get a move on. With a final lunge I ripped free of the fence, tearing my shirt and the skin on my back in the process. The wounds started to sting but we managed to run home without being caught and triumphantly presented the leaves to Mother the next day. She could hardly have failed to hear about the commotion the night before, but she accepted the leaves with a sly smile. We had all learned how to survive in the last four years, and sometimes we just had to take what we needed. Mother was perfectly able to survive without the leaves, but after so much deprivation we thought she deserved a treat.

The rice that we had stored was not enough to feed our family and though we could search for vegetables in the jungle, meat was in very short supply. We spent almost a year in our leaky hut and during the monsoon the rain was like an outdoor shower that covered the whole world. It rained every day for weeks on end, which created an opportunity to gather some much needed protein. Khay, Mei, Veng and I would go out and catch snakes, snails, crabs, frogs, or anything else we could. The snails and crabs apparently thought that no sane predator would be on the hunt in the midst of such a downpour. They came out of hiding and into plain view where they were easy to catch. The snakes were better to eat but harder to find, usually hiding inside the crab holes on the side of paddy dykes after evicting the original owner. The crabs seemed to take this in their stride and simply dug another home. When I found a hole I would shove my hand inside and grab anything I could feel. The snakes took a dim view of my intrusion and often sank their teeth into my fingers. Fortunately they were not poisonous and I was less afraid of their bite than I was of the leeches. I yanked the snakes out of the hole, twisted their necks to kill them and put them into a cloth bag along with any snails and crabs to carry home.

Khay would always range further than the rest of us, poking into any place that might yield something useful. One day he found and carried home a set of pots and bowls that someone had lost or abandoned. Eventually Khay had supplied, in one way or another, most of our household goods. He was a very good hunter and he was very persistent. If ever there was food or goods on offer, Khay would most surely see to it that our family got more than average. He always had a strong sense of self respect and when his older siblings made him angry, he would stuff all the pots and bowls that he had found with fresh cow dung so that no one else could use them. This never lasted long though, and when he cooled off he would clean them up and let the others use them again.

After some time had passed since the fall of the Khmer Rouge regime, Mother was confident that they would never return to power. They might still harass and kill people but they would not be able to steal the possessions of the entire population again. Rice was still being grown under a cooperative system, where each family had to do enough work to receive its share. The business of growing rice was backbreaking enough without having to plough the fields by hand, and most families kept a cow to help with the task. Using more of her dwindling gold, Mother traded for two bulls. The older bull was white, while the younger was a golden colour and very strong. The bulls represented a substantial investment and were very important to us all, not least because they meant a bit less heavy work for all of us children.

Mei, Veng and I were given the job of looking after the bulls and taking them out to feed each day. We would lead them to the land around the Vietnamese army base that had been built to counter the Khmer Rouge attacks in the area. We hoped that there we would have some protection from any wandering supporters of *Angkar*. We took nothing with us on these journeys, so we would tie the bulls to a tree and then wander around in search of lunch. We were also expected to find food to take home for dinner, so we dug up small, round, edible roots the size of an adult's big toe. They had a tinge of sweetness and a watery taste that also quenched our thirst.

We took very good care of our bulls and rapidly bonded with them, especially the young one who seemed unusually intelligent. One day we took the bulls on a fishing trip far away from home and were so intent on our task that we did not realise that it had started to get dark. When we finally noticed the deepening shadows we untied the bulls to return home. It was only then that we realised that we had no idea how to get home. Panic started to set in until it became clear that our young bull was pulling insistently in one direction and obviously impatient to be off. We let him loose and with a minimum of fuss he led us all the way home, stopping only when he had reached his favourite spot at home under the big tree. Clearly, this was a creature to be reckoned with.

Though we grazed our bulls near the army base, we were afraid of the *yuon* Vietnamese soldiers. There were a series of legends that had been told to children for decades, that the Vietnamese had stolen our land and killed our people. One story in particular was told and retold by Cambodians, growing more gruesome as time went on and it was passed from one generation to the next. It spoke of Vietnamese invaders who long ago captured innocent

Cambodians and buried them up to their necks, so that just their heads were above ground. They poured boiling hot tea on their victim's heads, all the while telling them not to spill the master's tea. The legend was a story that all Cambodians had heard and it took a long time to forget. After sharing a border there was bound to have been conflict between the two countries. Centuries of hate and suspicion between us were not easily erased.

Because of these lurid stories we were afraid of the base and kept our distance, ready to flee at the first sign of trouble. Something was odd though; the troops saw us and waved at us to come closer. They showed no signs of digging holes or boiling tea, and invited us to go into their base. They turned out to be very friendly, playing with us as if we were their own children. I assumed that they must be missing their own families. We could not speak each other's language and could not easily communicate, but that did not matter.

They sang songs and we clapped our hands and sometimes danced or rather, hopped around and tried not to knock each other over. We had lots of fun with the Vietnamese soldiers. The last time I remembered having any fun that did not end up with someone breaking an arm was when we had lived in Kratie. The troops gave us some of their food and it was the first time I had tasted bread since leaving Kratie in 1973. One soldier in particular took a liking to us. He got our attention and invited us into the base and then to his quarters, which might have been cause for suspicion but he did not seem to have an agenda. Maybe he was just bored or we reminded him of his own brothers and sisters. Maybe we reminded him of his own children.

We tried to communicate by the usual method of speaking slowly and loudly, but in the end we made do with hand gestures and pantomime. We did not manage to get much further than our names, discovering that his name was Minh. He gave us a packet of instant noodles each which caused no end of excitement. We ate them then and there without worrying about cooking them, and took the flavour sachets home to Mother for the family soup. She asked where we had got them, and after we told her she told us to get more of anything we could. Apparently she had never bought into the horror stories told about the Vietnamese, or at least had realised that her fellow Cambodians were every bit as capable of murder as anyone else.

We needed no encouragement. Looking after the bulls was rather dull work and anything that added colour to the day was welcome. We returned to the base as often as we could and if we spotted Minh we would call and wave to get his attention, hoping that he would let us inside the wire fence. In his tent we entertained him and the rest of his squad. Mei was mistaken for a boy at first because of her short hair and talent at whistling, with which she produced excellent versions of popular tunes while we sang along in Khmer. In return, one of the soldiers would play his guitar and another would overturn a metal bucket and use it as a drum. They would all join in singing and when we departed one day, Minh gave us a sack of flour to take home. Mother was delighted, and mixed the flour with water to make into bread-like sticks that she fried in fish oil. The result was very tasty to tongues that had been starved of flavour for so long.

After many visits, one day Minh was simply no longer to be found at the base. I hoped he had been transferred to a different base and had not been hurt or killed in one of the frequent harassing raids by the Khmer Rouge. We missed his smiling face and the bond that we had forged in that short time. We now knew that we could be friends with the Vietnamese and this feeling quickly became widespread as old prejudices diminished in the face of kindness of the soldiers.

The countryside was littered with so many land mines and booby traps that even walking across familiar fields meant taking your life into your hands. A wise person would follow someone at a distance if possible, discreetly treading where they had. If they were on their own or first in line then they followed the well worn paths that had been trodden many times before. I was a child and largely ignorant of military dangers, but one afternoon I was idly watching a cow some distance away as it grazed in a field. Khay was with me and said that the livestock in the field meant that it would be safe to search there for food. The cow took a step forward and the ground at its feet erupted in a geyser of fire and dirt; it had set off an elephant mine. The explosive was named as such because it was about the same shape and size of an elephant's footprint. The brutes were designed to destroy trucks and tank treads, so an unwary cow became a rain of blood and hairy specks of meat, scattered across a wide area. Khay had been cut off in mid-sentence by the blast, and his mouth hung open for a few seconds before he trudged off in another direction.

We did not try to retrieve the remains of the cow. It was not fear of the mines that held us back; it was simply that there were no pieces big enough to be worth scraping up and if there had been, we would have gathered all that we could. The avoidance of starvation was higher on our list of priorities than actual survival. It had never occurred to me that I was in danger of being blown sky high at any moment, but even if it had it would have made no difference to my behaviour. Death had become a creeping thing that claimed those not bold enough to run for their lives. It was better to risk dying quickly than to play safe and be sure of dying slowly.

We were very lucky. Every day my parents allowed us to take risks that would freeze the blood of any sensible person. They knew that if they tried to keep us away from harm then we would have all safely starved in each other's arms. They had to trust that Karma would keep us in one piece, together with a large amount of naivety, youth and ignorance.

While grazing the bulls, we came across a creek with crystal clear running water. There were small fish swimming around but as soon as they saw us, most of them moved upstream to take cover. We needed to figure out how to catch them to take home for dinner. We made a basket out of vines and I stood upstream waist deep in water while Khay and the twins tried to herd the fish towards me. I caught a few with each scoop of the basket and tipped them onto the dry ground. They flopped around for a couple of minutes before they started to die, but we could not afford to feel pity for any potential food source. The fish were only about the size of an adult's thumb, but there was no such thing as size restrictions and we took home everything we caught. I was too busy catching fish to have the time to dig for roots so I had gone without any lunch. I found some soft green jelly-like moss growing on the rocks in the creek, away from the direct sun light. It was not tasty but it was filling and kept my stomach from growling for a while. I ate too much though and had diarrhoea for the next couple of days.

One morning it was raining and the weather was so miserable we delayed taking the bulls out to feed. We waited for a break in the weather and it was only a couple of hours later than usual but Father seemed to be in a bad mood. The bulls had bells around their necks which acted as a security alarm for us. If the bell stopped clanging then we went to check their whereabouts. The bulls were still tied under the big tree where they slept every night but they were used to being out and about by then. They walked back and forth making so much noise from their bells that Father became impatient and untied the rope which let the pair of them loose. We had woken late and not finished our breakfast before they started to wander away from our house. We had to stop eating and run after the bulls, getting soaked in the process.

A few weeks later we woke in the morning and could not hear the noise of the bells. We leapt to our feet and sprinted outside in a panic, thinking that the bulls had been stolen during the night. They lay peacefully under their tree, chewing their cud and regarding us with the patience only a truly contented bovine could muster. Both of their bells though, were gone, stolen. Khay immediately knew who the culprit was. The previous day a boy from the village had wanted to swap his own bells for ours. Ours sounded better, had a more elegant design, and Khay knew a bad deal when he saw it, so he refused. If the village boy had known Khay better he would have saved himself the trouble and stayed in bed. Khay went straight to the boy's home and untied the bells from the cows without so much as a word. The boy took one look at Khay's face and did not dare argue.

There was an old mango tree at the edge of the village that was far too big to climb without risk. Mango trees were usually kept trimmed to a height that made the harvest easy. The lowest hanging fruit was high enough off the ground that a fall, at the very least, would break the bones of anyone too impatient to wait for the fruit to fall in its own time. The tree was heavy with ripe fruit and a number of people eyed the tree each time they passed. Everyone knew that after the next strong wind there would be a feast on the ground, ready for the taking.

I was woken in the dead of night by Khay. There was a storm howling outside, complete with lightning and squalls of wind and rain that lashed our leaky hut. Khay told me that we were heading to the tree to get a jump start on the rest of the village. There was no need to sneak this time, the roar of the wind was more than enough to keep everyone else inside with their windows shut tight. We arrived at the tree and I saw that the ground was covered by more mangoes than I had ever seen except at a market, knocked off the branches by the storm that still raged around us. It was still raining and we waited, huddled together with our backs against the tree trunk. I was cold and soaking wet but Khay was holding my hand and I stayed put, hoping the rain would stop. While we crouched there we froze as we saw a Khmer Rouge soldier walking towards us with his gun over his shoulder.

No one would be out on a night like that unless they were up to no good, with the exception of ourselves of course. If he had seen Khay or me, I had no doubt that he would have killed us, if only to make sure that we did not pass the information on to the Vietnamese army base nearby. The Khmer Rouge was no longer pretending that they had ever been working for the good of the people. They lashed out at anyone they encountered. They were like rabid dogs that attacked without provocation and could only be stopped with a bullet. I was terrified and might have made a run for it, but Khay tightened his grip on my hand and whispered to me to stay silent and still. I hoped the thunder would cover the pounding of my heart. The soldier passed within a few metres, but did not see us.

We waited for the storm to pass, shivering from the cold and our brush with one of the remains of *Angkar*. Finally, the rain stopped and we started gathering the mangoes into the bags that we had brought with us. There were too many for us to carry back home, so Khay stood guard over our booty while I took a bag full of fruit home and roused our elder siblings to help carry the rest. We all scuttled back to the tree and hauled the sacks to our hut, stashing them inside so that no one else would find them. We all agreed not to tell anyone about our night-time adventure and went back to bed with huge grins on our faces.

The next morning we passed by the tree as we took our bulls to graze. Other people were standing there with puzzled expressions, as they tried to figure out why hardly a single mango had fallen during the storm. Even more oddly, they were sure that there had been far more fruit on the tree the day before. There was little else to talk about in the village and the mystery was much discussed over the next few days. We kept our mouths shut, pretended to know nothing, and privately enjoyed the mangoes for the next week. We did give some of the fruit to the other family who shared our hut, but we made up some excuse that we had found them elsewhere.

Khay and I were always on the lookout for food to take home to our family. Harvesting of natural resources had taken on a competitive edge as every family strove to provide for themselves. It was still very possible to starve in Cambodia and we were not above a little petty theft if it provided food for just one more day. We saw that there were fish traps laid along the water canals that supplied the paddy fields. The traps were made in such a way the fish could easily enter from one direction but then could not swim back out. We found some traps that had caught some fish and decided to raid them. The area was flat and wide open with no trees, so it was easy to see people from a long distance.

Khay said he would keep a lookout for the owner and I should get the fish out. Keeping a wary eye out for leeches, I entered the water and put my right arm into the trap through the same hole the fish got in. I grabbed one of the wriggling creatures but then could not pull it out, and now that I was holding the fish I could not get my arm out either. Khay saw that the owner was coming and told me to hurry up. I was on the verge of panic when I let go of the fish and was then able to free my arm. When the owner arrived we were busy pretending to be looking for something else altogether. The man must have thought we were stupid as we picked masses of an inedible weed. Secretly, we observed how to untie and open the door in the traps to get the fish out. We were more successful the next time.

One day the village held a celebration that was unfamiliar to my family. That did not matter because we were not invited. Much of the old hatred had remained after the Khmer Rouge had been driven out. We were ethnic Chinese and originally from the city so we were barely tolerated and certainly not welcomed by the indigenous population. They got together and slaughtered a cow by the pond, afterwards burying the skin and head in a shallow hole. The next day Houy and I found it when we saw hundreds of flies buzzing around the mound of earth. We went to have a closer look and scraped away some of the dirt using our feet. We saw the cow's head, dug it up and shook off as much dirt as possible. Cambodia was a country where many things were eaten that other cultures would regard as untouchable. Even so, this was not normal behaviour for two young girls. Our view of what was potentially edible had been forever altered by the deprivation of the past few years, and fish had been our only source of protein for so long that even a shaggy and rather smelly cow's head became attractive.

The cow's head was full of maggot-like grubs, so we dunked it in the pond to wash away the worst of the wriggling white grubs. We carried the head home, each holding one of the short horns on either side. Mother was pleased even if it was not usual fare for us, as she recognised the amount of food contained in the brains, tongue and cheeks. She immediately set about producing a tasty meal out of the horrible thing, placing it into the fire to burn away the hair. Then she used an axe to split open the head; also not a standard cooking method. She boiled the pieces in a big pot with whatever vegetables we had at the time and we had our own feast that night. After its inauspicious beginnings, the head proved to be a delicious treat for the entire family. Any sort of meat was hard to come by, especially red meat, and we would normally have to exchange gold or rice to get any. We did not have enough surplus rice to trade for luxury foods that gave back fewer calories than they cost. Using gold was out of the question for that, and had to be kept for emergencies or durable goods that could be obtained in no other way.

In our constant search for food, my oldest sister Keang and I heard that the other village people were going into the jungle to dig up yams. When we asked if we could go along they said we could, but that the yams they were looking for were poisonous until they were correctly processed. This did not deter us and we followed them closely because they knew what to look for and we did not. As the yams were dug up the villagers discarded many as too small and not worth the effort. That did not matter to us because we were not going to go back home empty handed. At the end of the day we had a bag full of small tubers and only a vague notion of how to make them safe for eating.

The next day we peeled and thinly sliced the yams, then

took them to the paddy canal to wash out their toxic juices. We squeezed and rinsed the slices until the milky white sap was gone, then took the result home to dry in the sun. The plan was to use the yams to supplement our rice only if it began to run short. After the harvest, we had enough rice that we never had to run the risk that Keang and I had not actually managed to remove all the poison.

The harvest was completed but our hunt for meat continued. We saw that the field rats had been fattening themselves on the individual rice grains that had fallen from the heads as they were cut and carried. The rodents were normally lean and quick on their feet but now they had stuffed themselves until they were about the size of a man's hand. They were so fat that they could no longer run very quickly and so the chase was on. A slow rat is still a fast animal, and it took all of us children some time to corner one particularly tubby creature. Eventually we managed to grab the rat with our bare hands and took it home where Mother cooked it like she had the cow's head. She could turn the rat into a nourishing soup that would go further than simply grilling it over a fire. It was not much, but survival meant taking advantage of every single opportunity that crossed our path. Even a single chubby rat that had eaten more than was good for him was a welcome addition to our diet.

The rice planting and harvesting had been done in a communal fashion just as under the Khmer Rouge, but the grain would not be hauled off to parts unknown now. With the incentive of growing food for our family, Khay and I had moved quickly to plant seedling bundles in the paddy, far more quickly than most, if not all, of the adults around us. Months later the harvest had also been done as a group effort and again, Khay and I did at least as much work as any of the older members of the village. We cut the rice, bundled it, and carried it back to the village where we threshed it. When the time came to distribute the rice among the workers who had produced it, the village elders decided that Khay and I were only to get a child's share. To say that Khay was displeased would have been an understatement of truly epic proportions.

In fact he was livid, and this was a boy who would bury the family kitchenware in cow dung if an older sibling did not treat him with respect. The prospect of being robbed of his fair share of rice brought out four years worth of resentment at the injustice that had befallen us all. Now that he was no longer in danger of being summarily shot if he spoke his mind he was not to be denied. He created enough of a commotion in the central square of the village that the elders were forced out of their huts to confront him. They had never seen anything like it.

Khay demanded that we get adult shares because we had worked faster and had produced more than most of the adults. He articulated his case as if he was arguing for his life and flatly refused to back down. The elders were outraged that this 14-year-old *boy* was questioning their decision, let alone doing so in front of the entire village, all of whom had turned out to see the show. The villagers were appalled that Khay was acting this way, but also fascinated despite themselves. Nothing this interesting had happened since the vanishing mangoes of months before.

The debate went on for some time. It was probably for the best that when Khay swore at the elders he did so in Chinese, which they did not understand. The fact that he was right only made them angrier, and the rest of my family tried to calm Khay down. I did not bother; my brother was not going anywhere. Finally, the elders retreated to have a private meeting about this troublesome child and fifteen minutes later they returned to gravely deliver their final decision. Both Khay and I would receive adult shares of the rice harvest.

- 15 -

Fire

The harvest was over and it was obvious to Mother that it was time to make a choice: either stay in the village or go to the city. Father thought that it would be unwise to move and that we could remain happily where we were. We were relatively safe in the village and had enough food to eat, if only just. Any travel would be into the unknown, risking land mines, bandits, and contact with the disgruntled remnants of the Khmer Rouge. Every one of us was lucky to be alive as it was and after so many hardships, he did not want to take any unnecessary chances.

Mother did not see any future for her children if we remained in the village. The lack of a school meant that we would never get any sort of academic education. The people in the area would probably never accept us because of our heritage, and life would be an unending struggle. Mother had taken charge of our family, making most of the decisions while Father had taken a back seat. She did not want to take risks either, but soon her hand would be forced.

We had thought we were safe now that the Khmer Rouge had been chased into the mountains by the Vietnamese troops. We were wrong, and although *Angkar* might never again rule Cambodia, it was unwilling to simply fade away. It continued to make its presence felt by attacking random villages with mortar shells at night and then launching raids for supplies. Apparently the soldiers of *Angkar* thought it was beneath them to grow their own food and preferred to steal it from others. One night the flashes of explosions lit up the sky, coming closer and closer until the mortar shells were landing in the rice paddies behind our hut. They blew fountains of mud into the sky and left large craters in the ground that slowly filled with water. In the dark it looked like the earth was bleeding from its wounds.

My family had been sound asleep when we were awoken by the dull thump of the mortars being fired, followed by the sharp explosions as the rounds struck the village. We ran out of our hut and scrambled our way to whatever cover was available. It was not much protection, but we huddled next to the paddy dykes, which at least protected us on one side. We could only guess where the shells would land next and tried to keep the earth walls between us and the flying shrapnel. After the artillery assault flashes from the jungle marked the source of rifle fire, red streaks began to speed out of the trees. As we lay huddled on the ground, it seemed to me that a river of flame was tearing the sky apart just over our heads. I wondered if it would set the village ablaze and we would lose everything. Again.

We spent most of that night crouched in the mud, clinging to each other and flinching each time a shell landed. We prayed to whichever ancestors seemed most likely to help, that the Khmer Rouge soldiers would not stumble over us in the dark. It felt like forever to me, but eventually the assault ended and an eerie silence descended upon the fields. Even the insects seemed intimidated by what had just happened and were quiet, if only for a while. It may have been that after the thunderous explosions I just did not hear them. We stayed still for a while but finally I was convinced that the soldiers were gone and I stood up to go back to the hut. There was a *snap* as a bullet flew just above my head, trailing a tiny sonic boom in its wake and followed a moment later by the sound of the shot.

It was a parting gift from some disgruntled Khmer Rouge soldier, and I had been lucky one more time. I hit the ground and left it to someone else to decide when it was safe to go home. As I lay there I thought of nothing but survival and it was not until later that I wondered what our attackers had been trying to achieve. Had their goal ever been to create a new and better society, or was it just to inflict as much pain and misery as possible? The latter seemed more likely, since they were so very good at it.

Mother decided that enough was enough. We would leave the village and go to Kampong Cham where her own mother lived, and after that we would try to make our way to Phnom Penh. She still thought that Father's determination to return to Kratie had been a mistake, and she said that if he insisted on staying in the village then he could live there by himself. Father knew that she meant it and gave up the argument. If it had not been for Mother, I think that we would have lived there for the rest of our lives. I was happy to go; quite aside from the attack, we had never felt like we were a part of the community. We had not been invited to the regular village celebrations and everybody referred to us as the 'ethnic Chinese who lived under the big *Kor* tree'. Of course, there was also the small matter of the rice harvest.

We cobbled together a cart that the bulls could pull, although 'cart' would be a grand name for an A-frame of bamboo with no wheels. The top of the A was hitched to the bulls with the legs dragging behind on the ground, slowly wearing away as we went. We piled every possession we had onto the frame, including the

100 kilos or so of rice that was our share of the harvest, held in hessian sacks. Mother wheeled her bicycle, loaded with items that could not be squeezed onto the cart. Each of the children carried whatever household possessions we could. It was time to go, and so we began the first steps of a journey that would take years for some of my family to complete. It would take decades for others.

- 16 -

Downhill

We travelled for most of the day, and arrived in a sizable village several kilometres from the Mekong River. After asking around, Mother found temporary accommodation at a house owned by two widows and their two daughters. The nine members of my family stayed in the separate shed, rented for an agreed amount of rice each month. It would have been closer to go to Kratie, but we would need time to sell our possessions for the means to pay for river transport. Kratie had been taken over by the Vietnamese army, so there was nowhere to stay there.

In the year since the Khmer Rouge fell, private enterprise had returned in a rush, and by then several markets had sprung up. On offer were papayas, coconuts, fish, red meat, woven baskets, and anything else people had that might be of value. Other stalls sold deep fried bananas, roast sweet potatoes, sweets, steamed rice and vegetables. To us children there seemed to be an infinite variety of good things to eat, things that were a distant memory from another time and place. We could only stare at the displays while our mouths watered. Rice and gold were the only acceptable currencies and we would need what we had in order to continue our journey to the capital. We would stay in the village for several months while we tried to arrange transport to Kampong Cham, a hundred and fifty kilometres to the south along the Mekong River.

While we stayed in the village, we continued to walk our bulls into the fields to graze. One morning our favourite bull seemed to be out of sorts and it soon became apparent that he was seriously ill. This was the young, strong and smart one, who had led us home when we were lost in the jungle. He was a major asset to our family and a gentle and good-hearted beast, so we made every effort to help. He was not eating, even when we went out and cut his favourite leaves and grasses, bringing them to him as though he was a sick family member. There were no vets in the area but we had to do something, so Mother went to the market to buy some medicine, even though she did not know what illness the bull was suffering from. When she returned we tried to persuade our bull to drink the medicine, but he shook his head and refused to open his mouth. We had to hold his head and force open his jaws in order to administer the drug to our big friend.

Our bull died a day later. He may have had an illness that was inevitably fatal, or the medicine we had given him may have made things worse. For us it was like seeing our house burn down. Aside from our rice and Mother's shrinking store of gold, the bulls were all that we had of any real value. He had meant far more to us than just a farm animal or even a pet. We wept for several days, but we had to salvage what we could. We cut up the body of our big golden friend and exchanged the meat for processed rice at the market.

There was not much fun to be had in the village. I watched Mother ride her bicycle and wished I could too. I knew that if I could ride I could go further and faster than I was able to on my own two feet. My problem though, was that I was not quite a teenager and the bike was an adult sized version, built for a man. At the time, bicycles meant for women had a bent section between the front and back wheels that allowed a dress to be worn. Mother's bike was a solid machine with a straight bar, and even with the seat in its lowest position I could not reach the pedals. The only solution was to stand on the pedals with my leg through the frame, leaning against the cross bar. It was an awkward arrangement at best, and with my body bent into such an unnatural position it was too wobbly to pedal properly. I thought that if I could learn to steer then the peddling part could come later when my legs had grown long enough. Near our camp was an asphalt road that passed through town, then up and over a large hill. The answer was obvious: rolling down the hill would provide the momentum to practice steering. It seemed like a good idea at the time.

Khay came along for moral support and I wheeled the bike to the top of the hill, which did not seem too high or steep until we turned around. When I saw the road dropping away in front of me my heart began to pound and my stomach churned, as if they would prefer to be elsewhere. I wondered if I should have started lower down the hill, but Khay told me to get on with it and as I bent myself into position, it occurred to me that I had never actually seen him riding a bike himself. I glanced to one side and saw a large crow, perched in a spindly tree next to the road and staring intently at me. The bird gave a shake of its head as if to say 'Don't do it'. I was about to reconsider the whole plan, when Khay gave me a push in the small of my back and off I went.

I had never been in a car or on a train before, and within seconds I was moving faster than I had ever travelled in my life. I quickly discovered that the hand operated brakes did not work, but I managed to stay on the road for about one hundred metres before veering off into the waiting bushes. As I lay on my back, trying to decide if any of the limbs that were reporting pain were actually broken, the crow flew overhead and surveyed the scene with a disapproving croak. Plainly he did not appreciate good advice going unheeded. Khay dragged me out of the undergrowth, dirty, scratched and more determined than ever. Every day after dinner I returned to the hill until I could ride the bike in a straight line; I just made sure to start from a little lower down.

During the day, I sold various goods at the local market, similar to those I had carried door to door in our previous village. Each night I would pack garlic four cloves to a bag, or a spoonful of MSG at a time. I used a piece of wire heated over a candle to seal the bags. In the morning I would carry my basket to the market and squat in the scorching heat all day, trading items for rice. I had a place next to an old lady who was selling green *es cendol*, which is a sweet that looks like small worms, flavoured and coloured green with pandan leaves and served with thick coconut cream. The lady had fair skin and I thought that she was of Chinese ethnic origin. This was confirmed when I discovered that she knew a few simple Chinese words. She only had a few of her front teeth remaining and when she smiled the teeth she had left were brown and loose in their sockets. The full story of her hard life was written all over her face and hands.

When it was not busy we started to chat, sharing stories of the recent past that had heavily affected us all. Her name was Mrs Chang, although I always called her *ah'ee*, which is Chinese for auntie and was how children usually referred to any older woman as a sign of respect. She told me that I was a good girl for earning money for my family. I remembered eating the sweet she sold, having loved it when I had lived in Kratie. I wanted to have some but I was not about to buy it with the rice I had earned. I offered to exchange a bowl of her dessert for what I was selling and she agreed. It was every bit as good as I remembered and the flavour made me recall better times. This arrangement went on for weeks until one day she asked me if she could meet my mother. I really should have seen what was coming next.

After the market had closed for the day I walked home with Mrs Chang. I introduced her to Mother and left them to talk, since children were not allowed to be around when adults spoke together. It turned out that she could not have children herself and wanted to adopt me. She had a husband and one adopted son, but in Cambodia one child was not considered remotely enough. That evening my mother gave me away for the second time. Being the obedient daughter that I was, I went without question, but I did not have to like it.

She introduced me to her husband and her son, who both had the dark skin tone and facial features of the indigenous Khmer people. They were all very kind to me and shared whatever they had, which at the time was considerably more than my family. They had a roof for a start, and I had a place to sleep away from crawling insects, even if it was on the kitchen bench. Mrs Chang worked very hard and every morning she was up at 4am to make her sweets. She made them out of rice that she had begun soaking the day before, and then ground to a fine paste at night. I woke up when she lit the fire and its bright glow filled the room. She did not disturb me and I would turn to face the wall so that she did not see my eyes, red and puffy from crying throughout the night. At around 5am she would finish and make me a bowl of the *es cendol*, still warm and delicious. Then we would get ready to go to the market. We had to be there early or risk missing out on a good position.

Mrs Chang lined one basket with mosquito net off-cuts and filled it with *es cendol*, small bowls and spoons. The other basket held a bucket of water for washing up. She put a bamboo stick through the ropes holding the baskets and put it on her shoulder to carry to the market. This method of carrying goods was not particularly easy or comfortable and she had to stop several times along the way to rest. I went with her to the market to help her sell the sweets and we would remain there until all her stock had been sold or the markets were closed and deserted of people. We stayed for as long as it took because she could not afford to have any leftovers. The precarious nature of her business meant that she was always on the thin edge of survival and she would remain there for life. There would be no retirement for Mrs Chang, she would probably work until the day she died. On our way back home the baskets were filled with the rice earned from the day's trade and were not much lighter than they had been in the morning. I wanted to help her, so she let me put the stick across my shoulder. I could not walk though. I was too short and the baskets would only drag on the ground.

I noticed that Mrs Chang's husband never went to the market. He stayed at home gathering and chopping up wood with the help of his son, Boray. In the evening before dinner time I helped pick long melons by a pond with Boray. We did not have much in common and barely spoke. I missed being ordered around by Khay and directing my younger brother and sister in turn. The males in the household did not seem to do very much, not helping to cook dinner or prepare the sweets for sale the next day. Mrs Chang's husband was a traditional Cambodian man who left the cooking and cleaning to his wife, even though she was the one who earned their living. Mrs Chang was at the market all day and had to cook and clean at night, but she did it without complaint. I was miserable and missed being with my family, so a week later she decided to cheer me up by taking me back to visit them. When I got there I had so much fun playing with my brothers and sisters that when the time came to return, I flatly refused. This was out of character for me but I knew that my family was planning to leave the province, and if I did not act now I would lose them forever. That was the end of my stay with Mrs Chang, and my Mother's last attempt to give me away. I tried to avoid Mother for a few days so that she would not have the opportunity to send me back. I overheard her muttering that I was *reung kbal*, a stubborn head.

Mother decided that there was a better chance for at least some of our family to make it out of Cambodia if we split up. I did not know when or how she came by the idea, but I did know that she did not want all of her children to die without the chance to experience freedom. She felt that if even one of us found a better life then the risk would be worth it. It was a desperate act for her to send her children away from everything that was familiar and into the unknown. Only my three elder siblings were mature enough to strike out on their own, and Mother gave Keang, Huor and Houy a share of the gold she had kept safe for so long. They were aged 21, 20 and 16 respectively and told to make the journey to Phnom Penh ahead of us. From there they were told that they should each find a way to escape the country for the West. There was no plan to meet in the future, just to leave Cambodia by whatever means they could.

Two days later, my oldest brother and sisters left us after a tearful goodbye. They carried with them enough of the rice that we had grown or earned to pay for the boat tickets. The gold they had hidden on their bodies was only to be used when nothing else would do. We could not go to the river to see them off because we had to tie up some loose ends before we too departed the village forever. We watched them walk into the distance along the dusty road towards Kratie and wondered if our family would ever be together again. In fact we would meet Keang soon and Huor ten months later, but none of us would see Houy again for six years.

Now only Khay, me, Mei and Veng remained with our parents. Mother sold our remaining bull and her bicycle in exchange for yet more of the rice that we would need to buy our own tickets to the capital. Several weeks later we left the village and made our way to Kratie and the banks of the Mekong River, where we set up camp to wait for the next boat heading downstream to Kampong Cham. There was a noodle stall near us on the river bank and it had been literally years since we had enjoyed such a treat. A big pot of soup was kept hot to be served with the noodles and the smell made my mouth water and my stomach rumble. We children were unhappy that we had lost our big brother and sisters, so Mother decided to treat us and she exchanged some of our processed rice for a bowl of the rice noodle soup each. On the small tables provided for customers were bowls of chillies, fish sauce, MSG, salt, pepper and soy sauce that were to be added to the individual's taste. Khay hit upon the idea that we could make our rice exchange worth more by adding as many of the condiments to our soup as we could get away with. I had once heard that Western people say that 'less is more'. This was considered absurd in Cambodia where people knew that more was, in fact, more. We did what he told us and mixed in everything that was on offer. It tasted awful. Worse than raw cockroach, awful. We still ate every drop, but would remember the lesson forever.

The boat finally arrived at 6am and it turned out to be an elderly wooden craft that was about ten metres long and four wide. Propulsion was provided by a small diesel engine that produced far more noise, smoke and soot than the boat's sedate speed would have suggested. We left Kratie on schedule, which in Cambodia meant just as soon as the owner had packed every square inch of the deck with goods and passengers. On top were sacks of rice and other supplies piled to the height of an adult. In the bilges underneath went the chickens, ducks and pigs who obviously did not appreciate their quarters one bit. They squawked, quacked and squealed depending on their species, but all of them emptied their bladders and bowels in a sort of group protest. The smell under there was abominable, so the animals were left tied up while their owners rode on the upper deck. The amenities for people were hardly less primitive, with no toilets, water, or indeed anything else that we had not brought ourselves. We each had a small space to squat and if we wanted to stretch our legs we had to wade through the mass of people. This was the only option because, though it might have been easier to step over people sitting on the ground, it was considered highly insulting.

The boat made slow progress, made all the slower by stopping whenever someone wanted to get off. It also pulled into the shore if someone on the bank waved for a ride, with the owner examining the deck to see if it was possible to squeeze one more person on board. The answer was invariably yes. Maximising profits meant keeping the boat loaded to the point of sinking without actually going under. I was not concerned by the cramped conditions because this was the first time in years that I had a ride rather than walking with a heavy load. I enjoyed the scenery going by on the banks, the wind blowing in my hair and the fact that there was, just for once, nothing to do but sit back and relax. The fun was over all too soon though, and twelve hours later we arrived at Kampong Cham in the late afternoon.

- 17 -

Ice

As the boat docked at the side of the river there was no particular need to quickly get onto dry land, but that did not prevent people pushing and shoving each other in their haste. I was swept along with everyone else and found myself deposited by the water, soon followed by the rest of my family. We had come ashore next to the Kampong Cham market, which was about five kilometres from Grandmother's hut. The problem was that Father was unable to walk that far, and we still had two bags of rice with us that each weighed twenty-five kilograms. Mother found the nearest thing to a taxi service that was available and purchased a ride for both Father and the rice on a horse drawn cart.

These carts were the backbone of trade in the province because motorised transport was almost non-existent. They needed little maintenance and were fuelled by the plentiful grass that grew on the roadsides. Payment was again with rice and after the end of the Khmer Rouge a standard had rapidly come about, one that used a condensed milk can to measure out the appropriate amount. Condensed milk cans were readily available because fresh milk required refrigeration, which was almost non-existent in Cambodia. The canned version did not easily spoil after opening and as such was a popular substitute. Four full cans equalled

166

about one kilogram of rice and larger purchases, such as our boat tickets, were made with twenty-five kilogram sacks. Five kilograms of rice was the price of a ride for an old man and two sacks. The rest of us trailed along far behind the trotting horse.

When we finally arrived at my grandmother's house it was after dark and we were all exhausted by the long day of travel. She had been surprised when Keang, Huor and Houy had arrived on her doorstep several weeks earlier. They had stayed with her for two weeks before continuing on to Phnom Penh. She was positively astonished to hear that, aside from Bouy, we were all still alive. Though forewarned, when Father arrived at her house Grandmother thought she was seeing a ghost. She had been under no illusion as to what was going on across the countryside for the last four years. She flatly told us that with our ancestry, lack of the Khmer language, and lack of experience in country life, we should have all been dead a dozen times over. Mother said that it was all down to Karma, which Grandmother accepted as easily as if she had been told that night follows day. I still thought the idea was rubbish.

Grandmother's hut was fifty metres off the dirt road that led into Kampong Cham. Chickens roamed freely under and around the stilt hut with its single open room and thatched roof. Its floor was two metres above the ground, requiring ladder-like stairs at the front and back doors. The Mekong River was two kilometres away but during the monsoon the river swelled so much that it would reach up the slope to the hut. During particularly wet seasons the extra height was the only protection from flooding. A bamboo bed was under the hut on the dirt floor and it was here that people took shelter from the midday heat, to gossip and nap. Water came from a well nearby and had to be carried home in buckets.

The kitchen was underneath, with several clay stoves that looked like flowerpots, strategically cut to let air flow to the coal inside. The inside of the hut was almost exclusively used for sleeping, which we did on the bare bamboo floor. There was a plank of wood that could be placed across the inside of the compressed thatch door to lock it at night, although a single healthy kick would have torn the whole arrangement from its hinges. Grandmother lived with our Aunt Tek and her son Seam. Also living there was our Uncle Jev who had never married. Before the Khmer Rouge regime he had been in love with a woman, but her family had insisted on too much in the way of a dowry. Grandmother had not been able to afford to meet the demands, and so any potential for marriage was over before it began. Uncle Jev never became interested in anyone else, and would remain a bachelor for the rest of his life. There were ten people sleeping in the hut, or there would have been if there had been room. Uncle Jev was displaced from his usual spot, and had to sleep underneath on the bench that was usually reserved for the daytime.

Like many homes in the country and even in the cities, the hut had a variety of fruit trees growing alongside. There were banana, papaya, star fruit, milk fruit, water apple and lamut trees. All of these could be harvested at various times of the year. The tropical sun and plentiful water supply ensured that the fruit reached its peak of sweetness. With so many tastes and textures on offer there was never any problem in persuading us children to eat the produce, even if we had not recently experienced virtual starvation. Long ago I had come to my own conclusion that hunger was a very fine sauce.

We immediately set to work helping Aunty Tek plant her field with corn. The cornfield had already been cleared a couple of months before, but we still had to turn the soil over, ready for the new crop. It was laborious work because the soil seemed to contain more stones than dirt, and the task had to be done by hand. They had no animals to help with the process and I quickly began to miss our golden bull more than ever. With the ground prepared we used a pole with a chisel-like attachment at the end to poke holes into the soil, into which three kernels were placed and covered. Mei was prone to talking more than working and our aunt scolded her, saying that she would surely starve. Mei had apparently forgotten our recent history, and told her not to worry. She said that wherever she went people would give her more food than she needed.

Aside from Mei's ability to worm her way out of manual labour, hard work was no stranger to us. Our heavily calloused hands no longer gathered any blisters as we worked in the heat of the day. The planting tool had to be thrust deep into the soil so that the hole did not immediately collapse as soon as it was withdrawn. Mother came to help us and after several attempts she had nothing more to show for her efforts than a shallow dimple in the ground. She began to swear and mutter to herself, complaining of the hardships that beset her. Was this to be the story of the rest of her life, or would she ever get the reward that she felt she was owed by Karma? Mother had enough; it was time to ask an expert.

Mother called Mei to her side and asked her what she thought might be in store for our family. Ten-year-old Mei had never claimed to be able to see the future, but in the past she had occasionally made predictions that had seemed to come true. Possibly they were just the sort of thing that any child would hope was going to happen, but to Mother they had the weight of an oracle. Mother only sought such information when she was truly desperate, for she believed that to ask too often was to risk losing the gift altogether. Mei looked up and saw an airplane that happened to be flying by, and said that we would leave Cambodia 'on one of them'. At the time she did not actually know that airplanes had people in them and were used for anything other than dropping bombs. Mother took this as a sure sign that she was not destined to live out the rest of her days scratching away at the dusty ground. She stopped complaining and got back to work.

We stayed with my grandmother long enough for the corn to grow all the way to maturity. This meant that we got to find out that harvesting the corn by hand was tedious, hot and itchy. I rapidly learned to tell which cobs were ready to be picked by looking at the silk on top. When it was dried the corn was ready. Corn harvesting required more labour than that of any other farm crop I had ever helped with. The ears were stripped from the stalk and tossed into a bag which we had to drag with us and which grew heavier at every step. The bags were too heavy to carry out of the fields once they were full, so we transported them out of the corn field by tying them to the back of a bicycle and pushing it between two of us.

Once the corn was dry the husks and silk had to be taken off by hand. After that we removed the individual corn kernels, one at a time, with our thumbs. Each kernel had to be removed intact so that they could be further dried for storage. We boiled some of the kernels with a scoop of powdered lime to make the kernels burst, and then sold them at the markets with roasted sesame seeds and a sprinkle of sugar. All this work was worth it to increase the value of the crop, but it did not pay very well. It certainly did not pay well considering the many hours of work that was devoted to the crop, and it only paid in rice, not in hard currency.

One night we were all asleep after a hard day in the fields when there was a rustle at the back of the hut. It moved from the door to the point where the roof joined the wall, and we realised that someone was trying to break in. They must have known that my grandmother, aunt and uncle lived there but had not counted on another six people moving in. We started yelling and the intruders ran off into the night, hotly pursued by Khay who was outraged that anyone would try to steal what little we had. It was probably for the best that he did not catch them, because we did not know how many thieves there were. Khay had the heart of a tiger but he was still a young and skinny kid. The scene was repeated several weeks later with the same result, after which the intruders apparently got the message that there was nothing to be gained and gave up.

I decided that I wanted to earn some money, in the form of rice, for myself. This was partly because I would be able to spend it on whatever I wanted, and partly because anything would be better than working in the corn fields. I picked some bananas from the trees around the hut, cut them into bunches of six and put them into a basket. I rolled my scarf into a circle and used it to steady the basket on my head as I walked the five kilometres into Kampong Cham to the market. I sat for hours in the sun to sell my few bananas. It seemed like everyone else had far more goods to sell, both in terms of amount and variety. No one paid me much attention and by lunchtime I still had not sold anything. I grew tired of being ignored and I was not about to carry the fruit all the way back home. I began to yell at the top of my lungs, that I had cheap bananas for sale. Not just any bananas either, but the best and sweetest that could be had. It pays to advertise and people started looking at my offering more closely. Soon I had sold them all.

I had some rice to take home and was just preparing to leave, when a man pushed a cart past me, dripping with water. It left a trail behind him that stopped some of the ever present dust from rising into the air. On the cart were large blocks of clear glassy stuff that I had never seen before. I ran after him to get a better look and when he stopped I examined his wares closely, discovering that the blocks were cold! The man called out the name of his odd product: *teuk Kork*, which translated to 'solid water'. I had never seen or even heard of ice before. I had worked hard for my small bag of rice but I wanted to take some of the marvellous substance to Grandmother. She was always so nice to me and she seemed never to leave her house to find such a thing herself. I bought a piece of ice the size of a soft drink can and was handed my prize in a clear plastic bag, which I put into the basket above my head.

I walked the five kilometres back to Grandmother's hut through the heat of the afternoon, looking forward to sharing the cool treat with her. When I finally got home I found her cooking in the kitchen under the hut. I ran to her excitedly, took the basket from my head and showed her the present I had bought for her. The ice had melted. I opened the bag and found a single sliver the size of a thumb nail still intact. I tried to give it to Grandmother but she had seen ice before and refused to take it. She said that since I had worked so hard for it, I should have it. I thought that a substance so magical would be sweet and delicious. It was cold, as advertised, but otherwise tasteless and rather disappointing.

In another attempt to make some money, my aunt cooked soybeans and then fermented them in a way that the local people liked. She put the beans into baskets and carried them along the road to sell door to door. People would come out of their huts if they wanted our offering but the houses were all set back some way from the road, and it took quite some effort to attract attention. My aunt was the muscle and my job was to use my new found ability to shout as loudly as I could.

We only stayed in Kampong Cham for a few months. When the corn harvest was over, Mother was determined to move to Phnom Penh and seek the new life that Mei had predicted. We had largely run out of rice by then and had to use gold to pay for a ride in the back of a truck that had been used to carry dirt in another life. At the time, this was the main method of public transportation apart from the riverboats. The journey took three hours and just like our boat trip, we were packed in as tightly as possible so that the driver could make the maximum profit. It was just as well that we were, since the roads were rough in places and the tight confines prevented anyone bouncing around too much. Everyone on board swayed back and forth as one, bumping into each other and the metal walls as the truck negotiated the potholed road.

It might have been uncomfortable, but for us children it was also exciting because it was the first time we had ever been on a truck. Indeed it was the first time we had been on anything with an engine, apart from the boat that had brought us to Kampong Cham. We were high up in the air and the truck felt fast and powerful, although in truth it was an ancient contraption. I had almost certainly been moving faster during my first bicycle lesson with Khay. There were no toilet breaks, and any stops were only long enough for people to get on or off.

About thirty kilometres from Phnom Penh we had to cross the Mekong River near the town of Prek Kdam. The truck was driven onto a ferry and we were able to get off for a while and walk around the boat. The boat operators told us a story of a town called Neak Luong that had been razed to the ground by a B-52 strike in 1973. Apparently the Americans had been trying to halt the Khmer Rouge's advance toward the capital, but had only succeeded in killing or wounding many of the town's inhabitants. Twenty tonnes of bombs had struck in a line down the main street and killed almost one hundred and fifty people. I found out much later that there had been an attempt to cover up the mistake. The US Air Force attaché had reported that he *'saw one stick of bombs through the town, but it was no great disaster'*. The reports of minimal damage were shown to be a lie when Western reporters arrived in the area. American embassy officials had handed out single US $100 notes to the surviving residents for the loss of homes and loved ones. One note per family.

As we drew closer to Phnom Penh we saw more and more people on the roadsides, selling all manner of goods. Buildings became numerous and I stared out at grand houses, all protected by walls and gates. The walls were topped with Cambodian 'barbed wire', which consisted of broken glass set in concrete. It was an effective deterrent to potential intruders. In contrast to where I had grown up, trucks replaced ox carts and motorbikes replaced bicycles. Everything seemed to move at a hectic pace as people tried to make up for the past four years, a period in which any sort of normal life had been put on hold. The truck finally stopped in the centre of town. We jumped down and joined the fray.

- 18 -

Now or Never

The year was 1980 when we arrived in Phnom Penh, a place that had been known as the Pearl of Asia in the 1920s. Now it was home to two million people, all of whom had been traumatised to one degree or another by the rule of the Khmer Rouge. We saw billboards everywhere that had messages seeking to persuade people to accept the new government that had been set up with the support of Vietnam. Heng Samrin was an army general who had escaped to Vietnam during the rule of *Angkar*. He had asked for help from the Vietnamese government to liberate Cambodia. The Vietnamese had their own reasons for agreeing to help and probably thought that a sympathetic leader would keep a troublesome neighbour quiet for a change. The border disputes between the two nations had lasted for centuries, and finally the government of Cambodia was in Vietnam's debt.

Loudspeakers had been set up on many street corners and mounted on the back of motorcycles. They blared the party line, publicising the massacres committed by *Angkar* in order to gain support for the fledgling government. Mass graves were exhumed, containing hundreds, and then thousands of bodies. Many of those bodies were women and children, some with ropes still binding their hands behind their backs. The prison of Tuol Sleng was preserved as evidence of the atrocities of the former regime, and later opened to the public as a museum of horror. Compared to the recent past, almost any other leadership looked good.

It was in Phnom Penh that I first learned the name of the man who had led the Khmer Rouge for all those years. I could scarcely believe that a single person could be the source of so much pain and death. I wondered what had gone so terribly wrong with him, that he could do such things and think it was necessary. His infamy will live on without my help, and his name will be a curse forever. I will not sully my story by writing it here.

A new paper currency called the Riel had been introduced by the Heng Samrin regime, and as we got off the bus it seemed that everyone in sight was busy trying to earn as much of it as possible. Most transactions were being carried out in the new paper money and Mother grudgingly exchanged some of her gold for the new notes. Mother was all too aware of how easily paper money could lose its value overnight. Instead, she kept her assets in bullion wherever she could. Mother's gold had saved our lives more than once.

In the absence of an official postal service there were people prepared to travel around the country carrying messages for a small price. My parents had been able to contact my three elder siblings—who had gone on ahead—using these services. The messengers knew where to find Keang, Huor and Houy, and the apartment they had bought with the gold provided by Mother. The apartment was one room on the first floor of a building near the new market, *Psa Tmei*. The market had actually been there for some time and was a large concrete dome in the middle of Phnom Penh. In truth it had seen better days but it was awesome to me; I had never seen such a huge building before.

My three elder siblings had used some of their gold to buy wholesale clothing from Thailand. For several months Huor had been travelling by train between Phnom Penh and Sisophon. From there he had to make his way fifty kilometres to the Thai border to buy goods that might be in demand in the capital. Keang and Houy stayed behind and sold the items at the *Psa Tmei* markets. However, after a few of these buying trips Huor failed to return. Keang and Houy had waited until it became plain that he was not going to come back, then Keang decided that Houy should trace Huor's path in order to find their brother. Whether she succeeded or not, she was told to cross into Thailand and leave Cambodia forever to find a new life in the West. Houy was only seventeen and the youngest of the three so she did as she was told. Keang would remain in Phnom Penh and look after Mother and Father when they arrived.

Keang had been doing her best to earn new currency by selling the remainder of her Thai-made goods at the market. Mother immediately set to work doing the same, as did we younger children when we could. We had to stay on the edge of the market, hawking our goods from a mat on the street. We could not afford the levies necessary to secure an official stall inside the market itself. We were on the edge of legality, along with dozens of other people who were trying to scrape a living together. Because of this the unofficial sellers were often raided by soldiers or police, who confiscated our wares and kept them for themselves. The police were not paid a wage that allowed them to live, so corruption was effectively built into the system. There was no room for nobility or principles, everyone was out for themselves.

We were always on the lookout for the trucks and commotion that heralded the arrival of the authorities. At the first sign of trouble we would quickly pack up and hide until they had gone. Unfortunately the officers quickly changed their tactics and began making surprise raids in order to catch us before we could escape. I had always been brought up to follow the orders of authority figures and it was scary to defy them whenever they showed up. I would scramble to help snatch up our goods and then pretend that I was just a young girl out shopping. A girl who had just happened to buy fifty sets of underwear, for personal use of course. All around me were others in the same position. It would have been comical if our livelihoods had not been in peril.

A priority for Mother was to get her four youngest children into school. She found places for us at a nearby temple, which was where most schools in Cambodia were housed. Basic schooling was meant to be free for all children, and although our teachers were not meant to ask for extra payments, they, like the police, were not paid enough by the government to live. Our monthly fees, or bribes to be more accurate, were paid in either Riel or rice. At the age of thirteen I began to attend a proper school for the first time in my life, for a few hours a day. There were two shifts per day, in the morning and afternoon, but we could only afford one. We also had to buy uniforms, which consisted of white shirts and blue pants. Sandals were acceptable as footwear.

Discipline at the school was enforced with a long cane of bamboo, which was wielded with enthusiasm by the teachers. We lined up each morning to have our hands checked for cleanliness and to see if our nails were dirty or too long. If they did not pass muster, we would receive a painful rap on the fingernails. In class we had to sit with straight backs and pay attention, lest the stick swing into action. Caning was a common occurrence at school, but there were other distractions that could not be avoided simply by maintaining one's posture and the application of a scrubbing brush.

The school was built next to a temple, as was common in all areas of Cambodia. This meant that funerals were regularly held and these involved large processions of people passing by the classroom windows. Everyone involved wore white from head to foot, which was the traditional dress for mourning the dead. All had a square patch of black material pinned to their shoulder as a sign of respect. The patch would be worn continuously for a full month afterwards. Only the monks who oversaw the proceedings wore their usual orange robes. The spouse and children of the departed would shave their heads and cry as loudly as they could in a theatrical show of grief. This was to provide the deceased with a little extra posthumous 'face' and, by extension, also grant it to the immediate relatives. Gongs were rung and music was played at full volume through loudspeakers mounted on the vehicle that carried the coffin. The music was haunting at first, but when it interrupted my study for the third time in as many days, it began to take on the tone of a family of cats being drowned.

Cremation was most commonly used to send the departed on their way, but it was not the clean and clinical method used in Western nations. A pyre of wood was built and the body placed on top. A small amount of petrol was used to get things under way, and from there on it was a protracted and smelly affair. Inevitably the smell of burning hair would envelope the school as the cremation began, followed soon after by the scent of roasted human flesh.

Funerals aside, I loved school. I always arrived early and made sure I was in the front row, listening intently to every word my teacher spoke. I carried a small blackboard to and fro with two precious pieces of chalk, always white because coloured chalk cost slightly more. There was no paper, pencils or books and we would practice, write our answers and copy homework all on the book sized slates. The only subjects taught at school were reading and writing the Khmer language. Limited as the curriculum was, at least it was a start. As I began to learn, I could see possibilities for my future opening up before me. I thought that if I could gain enough knowledge, then I could get a proper job and earn enough money to gain my freedom. My life could truly begin.

I studied so hard and well that I was moved to the local equivalent of high school after four months, and began to learn maths and science. Some physical education was thrown in as an afterthought, but that seemed absurd to me. I had spent six years doing physical labour and did not want to waste my precious school time engaged in further exercise.

Khay had *lamors jeurng,* which roughly translates to '*itchy feet*'. He wanted to return to the village in Kratie province, to seek out and kill those who had anything to do with Bouy's death. We had heard that some survivors of the labour camps had exacted bloody revenge on their captors before they returned to their original homes. Khay would have done it too, but Mother put a stop to the notion and forbade him from returning. She said that killing people would not solve anything, and that making others suffer would not bring Bouy back. She said that Karma would take care of the culprits. She told us of her reaction when she had first received the dreadful news. The soldiers of the Khmer Rouge had informed her of what had happened and she had flown into a grief stricken rage. She screamed at them at the top of her lungs, crying and swearing that she had sacrificed everything to keep her children safe and that it was still not enough. The soldiers had backed off and left her weeping on the ground. Mother did not want to risk losing anyone else now.

Khay did not attend school with the rest of us children. We were running out of goods to sell at the market and as the eldest son still living with our parents, he felt it was his duty to provide for us all. He decided to go to the border and buy goods directly from the Thai merchants to bring back for us to sell, much in the same way as Huor had done before him. This practice was illegal under the laws set up by the new Cambodian authorities. With the economy just starting to function again, they wanted to control the flow of goods and exact sorely needed taxes. There was no doubt that self interest was also present, for the leaders could not pay themselves without a revenue stream. However, mere rules were not going to stop my brother for a minute and at the age of fifteen, Khay became a smuggler.

Mother gave him enough gold for a buying expedition and Khay caught the train to Sisophon. Each round trip took several weeks because the train was painfully slow, and even after he arrived there was much waiting to be done. The sellers who smuggled goods from the border to the markets in Sisophon arrived at random intervals and so Khay had to hang around until he found what he wanted. The alternative was to walk or buy a ride the rest of the way into Thailand, and then smuggle the products out himself. This was riskier and could add several months to the journey, but there was a greater room for profit. Khay was not one to shrink from a challenge and applied himself to his new trade. He hired people to use their bicycles to carry the goods he bought from the border to the train. This way he could maximise the amount he could bring back on each trip. If he could, he sold his wares to people from the capital who did not want to go all the way to Thailand themselves. If he found himself with stock that was not wanted in the immediate area, he would come back to Phnom Penh and we would try to sell it for whatever we could get.

While Khay was gone, Huor returned and told us the story of where he had been all that time. Huor had been at the border looking for goods to buy, and it had seemed to him that crossing into Thailand would not be difficult. It was understood among my family that if any of us got the chance to leave Cambodia forever then we should take it. He made it across the Thai border where he ended up in a refugee camp called Nong Chan. The Thai authorities gave him some food supplies and cooking gear and he settled down to wait for developments. He was surrounded by men, women and children who all wanted to escape to the West and leave the horror that their lives had become behind them.

After several weeks the Thai soldiers told the refugees to get into a convoy of trucks and that they would drive them to the United States. They did not mention just how far it was, and that there was quite a stretch of water between the mountains of Thailand and mainland America. Everyone boarded the vehicles without protest and they were driven into the night. The trucks stopped high up in the mountains in the middle of nowhere, and the soldiers told everyone to get off. The Thai soldiers robbed the people of anything of value that they could find, then told them to walk down the mountain at first light, back into Cambodia. The Thai government had problems of its own and did not want to deal with hundreds of thousands of hapless refugees. They had decided to get rid of as many as possible in any way they could.

In the morning, Huor found himself on top of a mountain in the Dangrek ranges. On one side of the mountain there was Thailand and on the other side lay Cambodia. Some people did not want to return to their homeland and some simply did not know which was which. In confusion some began moving the wrong way, down toward the Thailand side. The Thai soldiers opened fire, either as a warning or to make an example of people who they may have thought were being disobedient. Panic immediately broke out and people fled in all directions. Those running the wrong way were shot in the back and people stumbling down toward the Cambodia side had the Thai soldiers shooting at their heels.

It was later estimated that more than forty thousand Cambodians were taken into the Dangrek Mountains and abandoned, the worst case of forced repatriation in UN history. The Khmer Rouge had always been paranoid that the Thai Army would invade and had laid extensive minefields along the border. The Thais knew this and drove the desperate, frightened refugees into the danger zone. Mines began to detonate among the families and for many who had survived *Angkar*'s worst, their lives would end there. Many more fell prey to the bandits in the area. It is impossible to know how many thousands died on or near the Thai border. Huor made it out of the border region intact, but he gave up on the whole notion of escape.

Huor headed back towards Phnom Penh. He had managed to keep a small amount of gold well hidden. He used the last of it to buy a train ride back to the capital, determined to settle down and stay out of the sort of trouble that had killed so many of his fellow Cambodians.

Khay had been back and forth on buying trips to Thailand several times over the course of six months before his luck also ran out. While on the move Khay hid his gold in his clothes, because outlaws routinely robbed people and sometimes shot them in the process. His precautions were wise but ultimately useless. On what was to be his final trip he was robbed by guerrilla soldiers. Khay lost everything he had made on the trip, including his gold and all the goods he was carrying at the time. The bandits stopped short of taking the shirt off his back, but they did take the present my big brother had bought for me.

I owned nothing at the time, literally nothing. I had always wanted a watch of my own because it seemed to me that people who had a timepiece were successful. A watch was not necessary but it was a status symbol that most people did not possess. It did not matter that I had not yet actually learned to tell the time, I just wanted one thing of my very own that would make me feel special. Khay knew this and had bought me a watch in Thailand, but the bandits had taken it along with everything else.

Khay made it back to Phnom Penh, despite having no food or money. He never mentioned how he managed the journey, but it probably involved clinging to the roof of a train for twenty hours or so. Like Huor, he too was having second thoughts about a career in smuggling, and not just because of his recent run in with the bandits. The Thai troops stationed on the border were intent on discouraging refugees from crossing into their country, and they had amply demonstrated that they were not above shooting at people who were just trying to find a new life. Even before one got there, a gauntlet of booby traps and mines had to be negotiated to get through the jungle. Khay did not like his odds of long term survival if he continued to smuggle goods; however, when he arrived back home he discovered that there was a new problem.

The government had begun to conscript young men into the army while Khay was away. Mother was not going to let her son be sent into the ongoing conflict with the Khmer Rouge, who were now using guerrilla tactics to prolong the misery they had inflicted on Cambodia. She did not believe Cambodia would recover its stability and prosperity any time soon. We had heard about the string of refugee camps being set up by the UN along the Thai side of the border, especially for Cambodians seeking shelter. She thought it was worth any risk to get away, even after the horror of Huor's journey. She gave Khay some more gold and told him to get out of the country and not come back. He left the next day for the Thai border, but unlike many others who had made the attempt, he knew the way very well by now. He had little difficulty in crossing into Thailand, and once there he was placed in a refugee camp called *Khao-I-Dang*. He stayed there for several weeks and managed to contact Houy, who by then had been sponsored to the United States by a church group and had been living there for three months. In turn Huoy acted as sponsor for her little brother, and Khay's escape from Cambodia was finally assured. He was called for an interview with the American officials, and promptly disappeared.

While Khay had been gone, life for us in Phnom Penh had been getting harder and harder. Each day Mother would rise early and take Mei and Veng to the market to try and sell her dwindling supply of goods, to people who usually did not need or could not afford them. She knew that she would not be able to make enough money to keep us all fed for much longer, and grew increasingly distressed. Once more, Mother went to Mei for a prediction as to what would become of our lives. Mei told her not to worry, for brother Khay would come to get us and we would all go to the West. Mother asked how soon this would happen and was told in a few weeks, Khay would be there. Mother knew Khay was gone for good and began to doubt her youngest daughter's psychic abilities.

One day there was a knock at the door of our apartment and Mother went to see who it was. Khay stood outside and Mother simply asked: 'What the hell?' When it came to the point, Khay had decided that he was not going to leave without his family and had returned to take us all with him. Mother tried to argue but he flatly refused to leave on his own. Refusing one's parents was not the done thing, but she knew that he would not be denied. Khay and Mother discussed the issue for several days and finally came to the conclusion that Father was too old to walk all the way to Thailand from the last train stop. It would greatly increase the risk to everyone to move at the painfully slow pace that was all Father could manage. The territory we would have passed through was seeded with mines and nimble feet were needed for safe passage. They decided that I was also too old to accompany them, or rather, just old enough for a different and altogether more sinister danger. If I was found in the jungle by the bandits that roamed the area then I was of an age where I would have very likely been captured, raped and killed. Instead it was decided that I would remain in Phnom Penh and look after Father.

Mother was absolutely determined to escape Cambodia. Her country had been drenched by the blood of genocide and she could see nothing but more suffering with no hope for the future. She had little trust in the new regime and their already corrupt attempts at restarting the economy. Mother left most of her remaining gold with Huor to look after us and as capital to do business. She hid the gold that she would be taking with her at the bottom of a plastic jar that was filled with lime paste. It was, after all, a strategy that had worked well in the past. Except for that solid currency they carried little else with them; no extra clothes, food or even water. Mother said goodbye to me, but I did not comprehend that she was never going to come back. I had been told what was going on but I just could not believe it. I clung to a naive assumption that they would all be back again in a few days. Mother left with Khay, Mei and Veng. They vanished from my life for the next four years. Again.

- 19 -

Lucky Numbers

I never paused to feel sorry for myself. Mother was gone and I had to look after Father. I suppose that I had been doing as I was told for so long that it had become instinct. People came and went, and I never had any say in the matter. I would have preferred it otherwise, but it seemed that was simply not how life worked. Father told me that if I had raised a fuss Mother would have relented and taken me with her, but obedient child that I was, I had said nothing. Maybe one day I would answer to only myself, but it seemed a distant prospect.

Father and I lived with Huor and his wife Kim. I continued to attend school but I had to do more work at home to look after Father, such as fetching water from the ground floor and doing our laundry. It was heavy work to carry the buckets of water up the stairs and the whole process took several hours a day. Every time I emptied my bucket into the concrete storage tub on the first floor, I then had to come back down the stairs and wait my turn in a queue of twenty to thirty people for another turn at the tap. Only the people on the ground floor had running water in their homes. The pressure in the pipes was not high enough to push the water to the higher levels, and some people made a meagre living carting water up the stairs for people who could afford that luxury.

There was a kitchen at the back of the apartment next to the bathroom and toilet. These rooms had no windows and were almost pitch black. We cooked our meals by the dim light of a candle and used a coal fired clay pot stove for heat. There was no ventilation and the smoke from the burning coal continually covered everything with a grimy layer of soot. The candles only added to the murky air and I was jealous of our next door neighbours. They were better off than us and had a kerosene lamp to light up their kitchen.

I hated the bathroom most of all. It was pitch black in there and because a shower involved splashing water everywhere, it was also permanently wet. The lack of light and ventilation meant that slime grew on the walls and floor and it was my job to scrub it clean every day. The floor was slippery, which made it treacherous to walk on with only a candle providing a flickering light. The pipe that drained the floor ran through our downstairs neighbour's bathroom and it was rusted away near the ground. The same pipe also drained the two floors above us and this meant that whenever anyone upstairs bathed, water would splash into the ground floor bathroom too. The people downstairs took to blocking up the pipe with old rags to prevent the water pouring into their home. We had to ask nicely to persuade them to remove the obstruction so that we could bathe without flooding our own house. They seemed to use their position to get people to do what they wanted, and if tempers ran high then they always held the trump card. We did not have enough money to contribute to repairs and no one else was going to pay, so the stand-off remained the entire time we lived there. Mercifully, the toilet drained via a different pipe.

Huor's wife Kim had been born in Cambodia but her family had moved to Vietnam when she was a teenager. Through chance she had avoided the years of chaos and had never faced the sort of struggle that my family had. Her family had returned because they had capital to begin a business, and very little competition among the dazed population. Kim became pregnant soon after Mother left and she decided that in her delicate condition she should not be doing housework. I was dubious, for I had seen many people working long hours in various stages of pregnancy, and it had never seemed to bother them. Possibly the presence of the Khmer Rouge had been motivation enough. One day my sister-in-law had had enough of the house chores and she decided to leave and live with her mother. Huor followed to live with her, so Father and I were left alone.

It was obvious that I could no longer afford either the time or the money to go to school, and my education came to a sudden halt. It was a crushing feeling to have my one hope for a future taken away from me. I had heard once that the only way to hurt a person who had lost everything, was to give them back something broken. Losing school felt like that to me and it was particularly cruel now that I had been granted a taste. Education was a bet that could not lose. All you needed was the small price of a ticket and it would guarantee a win that would provide a decent living. The price was small, in fact tiny by most standards, but it was still too much.

I borrowed books from a friend's uncle who lived nearby, and kept trying to educate myself. The books were mostly novels but at least I could practise my reading skills. I dreamt about school at night and I wished I could go back. Every day I watched the children go by, dressed in their blue and white uniforms and carrying their books. Every day their talk and laughter faded into the city noise and I turned back to my chores.

I missed my mother every moment, but never so much as one day when I came home from shopping, went to the bathroom, and found that my pants were wet with blood. I had no idea what was going on, and could only think that the leeches that had scared me for so long had managed to crawl inside at some time in the past. How could that be though? I had not been in a flooded rice paddy for almost a year, and surely they could not have hidden all that time. I cleaned myself and used a bundled up pair of pants as a makeshift dressing.

I had never spoken to Father about such things, and lived in terror for several days until Keang eventually came to visit. I dragged her to one side and told her my problem. She laughed and said that I was becoming a woman, and that the bleeding was just a part of that fact. It turned out that my period had been delayed for several years because of starvation and constant work. I bought underwear for the first time in my life, to hold in place some pads I made out of clean material.

Father and I needed money to live, and I had to work out how to earn it. I had to look after Father and care for him on my own since he could no longer support himself. My aunt from Kampong Cham wanted to do business with me, buying and selling rice grown in the provinces to the city people. Mother had left each of us some gold and Huor was keeping my share safe. My aunt asked me to get my gold from Huor and we would use that capital to begin. Huor discussed it with his wife and decided that I was too young. They thought that I did not know what I was doing and would probably lose it all.

It was fortunate that the lessons of *Angkar* had not lodged in the minds of the Cambodian people. There was still a taste for gambling that I did not possess but could still take advantage of. I decided to sell lottery tickets. A local lottery had started in Phnom Penh even before the main fighting had stopped, and it was a popular way for people to try to improve their circumstances, if they were more inclined to dream than to work. I thought the notion of paying money with only a small chance of a payout was ridiculous. Why could people not do simple math? It did not stop me from taking advantage, and with the lack of communications in Phnom Penh there was a profitable niche to be filled, one that did not need much in the way of start-up capital. During the Chinese New Year I had received some money from relatives in the traditional red envelopes and I had saved most of it. These gifts were usually used by children to treat themselves, but I used mine to begin my new business.

All I really needed was a flat board and a stool, and the seat was optional. Father helped me to find some scrap wood and we managed to put together a board about one metre on each side, complete with a stand. It resembled a rickety easel, but it would do the job. Some nails were hammered into the wood and rubber bands stretched between them. I travelled across town to the lotto office and bought books of tickets for the next draw. I displayed the books of tickets on my board where they would be held in place underneath the rubber bands. The idea was that I would act as an agent and sell the tickets on the street to people who did not want to go all the way to the office themselves. The unsold tickets and the stubs from the sold ones all had to be returned to the office to prevent cheating. I would keep a small cut of the price of tickets I sold, and the lotto office would refund any leftover tickets the day before the draw.

I woke at 5am every morning while the sky was still dark and made my way to secure a spot by the road that led to the market.

I sat and waited until the sun rose so that no one else could take my position, then stayed there in the sun all day long, hoping that people would buy my tickets. I dozed in the heat of the day, dreaming that I had a permanent stall in the shade of the market. Each lunchtime, Father would come and watch over my board so that I could get something to eat.

Once a week, the lucky numbers would be chosen using the time-honoured method of drawing ping-pong balls from a rotating cage. I would attend the draw and take note of the numbers, then buy the dozen or so new books of tickets I would need for the next week. I took care to try to get the same numbers each time, for Cambodians are nothing if not superstitious. My customers insisted on playing their own numbers each week although they did not seem any better on average to me. I then paid for a ride on the back of a bicycle, returning to the market where Father would be waiting to keep my usual spot from being taken. I would write the winning combination onto strips of paper and sell the information to anyone who wanted to know the results. Writing out the numbers by hand was laborious, even after someone told me about carbon paper and I bought a single sheet to double my output. If a person had a winning ticket with a minor prize, I would offer to buy the ticket for 90 per cent of its value and save them the journey to the central lotto office. Then I would cash in the ticket and keep the profit.

In this way I supported my father and myself for nearly two years. I only managed to make just enough money to survive. If I ever fell ill, even for a single day, there would be no money for medicine or food. Many, many people were in the same position across the city. At that time there was nothing else in my life. No holidays or anything to mark one day from the next. At the end of each day, I would take my earnings and buy cheap cooked food to take home to Father for our dinner. Father often complained about the food. He did not like traditional Khmer food with its odd flavours and textures, but I could not afford the more expensive Chinese food. I was busy every day, but I just relived the same week over and over. Each night after dinner I listened to songs from the neighbour's radio. I dreamed of owning a bicycle and a radio, but could never afford to buy them. I wondered what had happened to Mother and wished she had taken me with her. It never occurred to me that she might not have made it over the border. Mother could face down a tiger. She could do anything.

Huor's wife had given birth and Keang had also started a family. It was hard for me to make enough of a living for both myself and Father, and the income I was earning was too precarious to be relied upon in the long term. Huor and his wife came to a decision: they would use all of the gold that Mother had left behind to get Father and me out of the country forever. The new government knew that if the borders were opened then much of the traumatised population would immediately leave. Any attempt to escape was considered an act of betrayal and was punishable by imprisonment. For thousands of Cambodians such threats did not matter. The Khmer Rouge was still in the jungle and the nightmare could return as suddenly as it had disappeared. We had received a letter from Mother that a country to the south called Australia had accepted her, Khay, Mei and Veng. She said that it was safe there, and that was all that really mattered.

We could not take the train towards the Thai border like Mother and the others had done. That journey involved a walk of several days through dangerous country and was only possible for people in good condition. Father, who could now barely walk, was incapable of making the crossing. He would have faltered and died along the way and I would have been left alone and at the mercy of the bandits in the area. Our only option was to use an 'agent', a man that would later be called a people smuggler.

In 1983 Huor agreed on a price of ten *damleung* (375 grams) of gold for a one-way boat ride out of Cambodia for Father and me. He paid five *damleung* initially, with the balance due when Father and I were safely delivered to our destination. That just left the question of trust, a commodity that was in exceedingly short supply at the time, and which would remain so for decades to come. What was to stop the captain of the boat from dumping us over the side and merely saying that he had fulfilled his side of the bargain? The thought had occurred to others, and there was a standard procedure. Father would sign a piece of paper in a specific way, one that only he and Huor would recognise. The agent would have to produce this signature to claim the rest of his money from my brother.

On our final night in Phnom Penh, we said goodbye to Huor and the next morning we left our dilapidated but relatively secure home. Carrying only a single change of clothes, we set out on what I hoped would be our final journey. The agent instructed us to not ask any questions and to keep our mouths shut. We were taken by bus to the sea resort town of Kompong Som, now called Sihanoukville, where the agent had arranged for us to stay with a fishing family while the arrangements were made for the boat. We stayed by the shore for several days and it was the first time I had ever seen the ocean. I had not even been aware that sea water was salty and I could scarcely believe that there was such a thing. I kept dipping my finger into the water and tasting it, remembering the hundreds of boring meals I had eaten in the past that sorely needed a dash of salt. The water appeared to go on forever, although it did not seem possible that the peaceful country of Australia could be very far beyond the reach of my straining eyes. Surely the boat would quickly take us there.

After several days, the agent took us to a dock and left us with another male passenger in his thirties. The boat arrived shortly after, and my first sight of it made me wonder if Father would decide to back out of the deal. The vessel looked like it might lose the struggle to stay afloat at any moment. Surely this dilapidated wreck could not take us far. It was in worse condition than the riverboat that had taken us from Kratie to Kampong Cham, and there were no waves to speak of on the Mekong River. Father knew that this was our one and only chance to leave though. We would not have either the money or the opportunity again. There were few ways to leave Cambodia and the others were effectively closed to us. It was now or never.

We boarded the boat and were taken below deck into a dank and dark space that would never ordinarily accommodate passengers. We had to remain hidden because if anyone from the government saw us on deck we would be returned to Cambodia and probably placed in prison. A final hazard was the pirates that were common in the oceans around Asia. A fishing boat that was visibly carrying passengers would have been easy prey. The bandits would think that people who could pay the exorbitant rates demanded by the people smugglers would surely have some extra money to steal.

We had nothing though, literally nothing, that would interest a bandit. We still had to remain out of sight, apart from quick toilet breaks in the dark of night and sometimes not even that. The three of us spent the entire journey squatting in the bilges of the boat, ankle deep in water and without enough room to sit down. There was no chance whatsoever to lie down and sleep. Every afternoon the waves would build up and pound the small vessel with walls of water that were as high as the boat itself, so sleep would have been impossible anyway. It was frightening every time the bow of the boat rose into the sky and then plunged down the other side of the swells. A boat ride down the Mekong with a load of disgruntled livestock was positively sedate by comparison. I do not know how many days and nights we squatted inside that hot, cramped and stinking little boat. I told myself that it would be worth it, if only we could find a place to live in peace.

- 20 -

Other Roads

With the decision to leave the country made, Khay led Mother and the twins Mei and Veng to the train, out of Phnom Penh and toward Battambang. After so many buying trips to Thailand, he knew the route well. They stayed there with a family for one night, and the owner of the house told Mother that she would have trouble at the checkpoints. Because of their mixed heritage, Mei and Veng looked Vietnamese and this made them a target for the local authorities. Mother also heard news of the atrocities inflicted by Thai soldiers on refugees in the mountains between Cambodia and Thailand. Mother knew the assorted dangers of attempting to cross into Thailand, but she calculated that at least some people would get through. Anything, anywhere, had to be better than the shattered remains of Cambodia, so she pushed on.

Khay knew that anything he could take to sell once they reached the Thai refugee camps would greatly ease their life. He bought five kilograms of dried fish and carried it tied to his back with string.

The next morning he bought them rides on motorbikes towards Sisophon, which was the last town of any size before the border. Khay went on the back of one motorbike, with Mother and the twins on the other. That meant that there were four people altogether on one small machine. In Asia at the time, anything up to six people at once was not uncommon.

When they reached the checkpoint close to Sisophon, Khay pretended to be a local boy on his own and the local soldiers waved him through without difficulty. As predicted though, Mother and the twins were stopped. Even though the Vietnamese army had freed Cambodia from the Khmer Rouge, the old hatred ran deep and the twin's faces marked them as the enemy. Of course there was no reason for the soldiers to prevent someone from taking Vietnamese children *out* of Cambodia, but they were hoping for a bribe. With Mother, they never stood a chance.

Mother maintained at great length that she was just trying to take her grandchildren to see their mother, who lived in Sisophon. The soldiers were having none of it. They had nothing better to do than try to shake down anyone they could for whatever they could get. After several hours of begging, Mother changed tactics and switched to a loving motherly tone. She spoke as if the soldiers were her own children and called their bluff. She said that if they would not let their Mother pass, then she would just have to go back the way she had come. She gathered the twins and turned around to do just that, at which point the soldiers finally gave up and let her through the checkpoint.

Khay rejoined them and they made it to Sisophon where they stayed for several nights. There was a pause in their journey in which Khay searched for a partner to help with the expedition, and then arrange to act as a smuggler for three other families. The arrangement was as harsh as it was necessary. Khay would receive half his money before they set out from Sisophon, in return for which he would give them instructions on where to go and what hazards to avoid. A group of families together would be an easy target for the bandits in the region so it was mandatory to split up. They would all meet up at several points along the way where they would be given their next set of directions. Anyone who did not make it to the rendezvous points was on their own.

It was still about fifty kilometres to the Thai border, and Mother and the twins left Sisophon on the back of an ox cart. Meanwhile, Khay paid for a ride on the back of a motorcycle so that he could scout the way ahead. He was not there to help when Mother was ambushed by bandits and dragged deep into the jungle along with her two youngest children. It was fortunate that Khay was not there as he would most certainly have resisted and would have ended up dead. Mother and the twins were searched from head to toe but the thieves could not find anything of value. The men were Khmer Rouge guerrillas and fully capable of any level of violence. They held a gun to Mei's head and threatened to kill her on the spot. Mei spoke to Mother in Chinese so that they would not understand, telling her now might be the time to relent and give the bandits what they wanted.

Mother knew that the small gold pendant that she carried would make a huge difference to their lives in the refugee camp. She knew that a small amount of hard currency could be the difference between life and death and begged the bandits not to hurt her children, but they simply did not care. Finally she dug the pendant out of its hiding place in the bottom of her lime paste container. It was the pendant that her own mother had given to her on the day she married, and it was her very last possession of any value. She handed it to the armed men and they left Mother, Mei and Veng in the jungle unharmed.

On the way back to the road, Mother saw another guerrilla soldier in the act of raping a teenage girl who was about the same age as me at the time. She could do nothing to help and had to think of the safety of her own children. She knew then that her decision to leave me behind in Phnom Penh had been the right one. She knew that she would not have been able to live with herself if she had witnessed her own daughter being brutalised.

When they got back to the road, the ox cart was long gone. The owner had only been paid for a ride, not to risk his life. He could not have resisted the kidnapping of his passengers and had not stayed around to see if they re-emerged from the jungle. He had probably not expected them to. With no money to try to buy another ride, Mother and the twins started walking towards the rendezvous point where Khay would be waiting. They had no food or water and did not know exactly how far they had left to travel. They began to suffer from dehydration and their cheap sandals quickly disintegrated, leaving them barefoot and with many kilometres still to travel. Mother kept walking, leading her tired children on until they were finally spotted by Khay and re-joined the members of his people smuggling tour group.

By then, night had fallen and Khay was uncertain of the direction he had to go. He climbed a tree so that he could see the stars above the dense jungle canopy and re-orient himself. By now their growing thirst was becoming a desperate need and they drank from a muddy puddle by the side of the road. Mother started to hallucinate and see things in the darkness that were not there. She saw what she thought was a pool of water that had been used by someone to wash clothes and still had soap bubbles floating on top. She stepped into the pool to cool her aching feet, but it was actually the hot coals and ashes of a recent camp fire. Her feet were burned and blistered before she could scramble to safety. The burns were not extremely bad but there was a long way to go, which had to be travelled on foot, and they had no time to wait for Mother's feet to heal.

The border was not far away by then and the group split up once more for the crossing. A long, steep and high mound of dirt had been constructed along that part of the border to make it easier for the Thai soldiers to spot anyone trying to cross into their country. There were patrols up and down the mound but Khay knew that they could be avoided if their timing was right. At the crucial moment Veng and Mei ran up the slope and down the other side to hide in the grass. Khay pushed Mother up the hill but was unable to help her to walk down. She had to slide down face first and crawl into the grass with the others.

They were in Thailand, but far from safe. The Thai government did not want them there and the soldiers or police would shoot anyone they found loose in the countryside. Once inside the refugee camp they would be off limits, but until then they were in a deadly game of skirmish where only one side had guns. It was still a considerable distance to the refugee camp that Khay had been in earlier, and Mother could no longer walk. The group had reformed after the border crossing and now a decision had to be made. There was a low mountain range that had to be crossed, and Mother was slowing the group to a crawl. She said that she could go no further and that they should leave her there and then, but Khay flatly refused to abandon her. He sent the others on ahead with his partner, after telling them how to break into the refugee camp. Khay made his partner promise to take the twins with him to the United States and meet with Houy. He remained with Mother to try to help her complete the rest of the journey.

Khay and Mother were now on their own, but managed to struggle to the top of the mountain range through the jagged rocks. Mother's tender feet were badly cut by the sharp edges, but there was no other way. When they reached the summit though, they found a Buddhist temple whose monks were sympathetic to their plight. They were given food and water and were able to rest there in safety for several days before going on. After descending the mountain Khay and Mother managed to avoid the authorities, but her burned feet were still very painful and her strength again began to fail. Their pace slowed as Khay supported, carried and finally dragged Mother to the very perimeter of camp *Khao-I-Dang*.

Three fences of barbed wire stood between them and the relative safety of the detention centre. There were watch towers at intervals along the fence, and at night spotlights would sweep the open ground as the guards searched for intruders. The security was mostly aimed at keeping people out rather than in. Mother and Khay lay in the grass waiting for their opportunity. Khay knew the weak points and after the shaft of light from the closest tower had gone by, he dragged Mother through the fence and into a patch of grass. They lay there with pounding hearts as the light passed over them, but they were not seen.

Draped over the fences here and there were the dead bodies of people who had been seen and shot, as they made the same short but dangerous journey. They were left there to dissuade just the sort of thing Khay and Mother were attempting. Another fence was crossed in the same way as the first and now the exhausted pair lay before the final barrier. This fence was better made and strung more closely to the ground so it had to be stretched upwards before someone could crawl underneath. Khay heaved at the wire and eventually made a gap big enough to stuff Mother through, although they were both badly cut by the barbed wire in the process. They collapsed on the ground inside the camp, safe at long last.

The next morning Khay found that Mei and Veng had managed to run the same gauntlet through the fences, with the help of the other families and Khay's partner. Without a family member to keep a close eye on them the twins had been at constant risk of being left behind. At every rest stop Veng would collapse into sleep the moment he lay down, and Mei had to force herself to stay awake so that they did not miss the call to move on. Mei would drag her protesting brother to his feet and pull him along at the tail of the group. They stumbled on and had finally made it to the camp. After avoiding the guards and wriggling through the fence wire, Veng had been taken captive by some of the other refugees who demanded ransom. She had none to give and dragged her brother out of the grip of the man who was holding him, and the pair ran for their lives. They were profoundly relieved when Mother and Khay arrived several days later. Mei and Veng told Mother that if they had known what the journey was going to be like, they would have refused to leave Phnom Penh.

Mother was unable to walk for a month after her arrival, as her feet slowly healed and she recovered some of her strength. Khay sold the dried fish that he had hauled all the way from Cambodia, collected the last of the money owed to him, and set about contriving plans to make more. Flushed by his success, my sixteen-year-old brother broke out of the camp yet again and returned to Battambang to repeat the performance. He smuggled yet more people over the border and into the camp, but his flourishing business was dangerous. Mother knew that if he kept at it, his luck would run out sooner rather than later and she would lose another of her children for good. As Khay made plans for his next escape she told him that if he went ahead, she and the twins would follow him and they would all die together in the wilderness. Maybe she was bluffing, but Mother had always been better at cards than Khay. This time he remained in the camp.

Mother had to register their arrival in the camp if they ever hoped to be accepted into another country. They presented themselves to the camp administrators who signed them in with weary resignation. It was no surprise that yet more people had appeared in the night as if by magic and despite the best efforts of the guards. Now that they were official refugees, Mother contacted Houy in the United States and she began the family sponsorship process over again. This time there were four people rather than just Khay, and the American officials were reluctant to allow them easy entry.

The Australian representatives had no such qualms, and offered places to Mother and her children. The American officials then had a change of heart and also offered them all settlement in the United States. They said to Mother, 'Don't you want to be with your daughter?' Mother was thoroughly irked by the Americans' vacillating and decided that if they did not want her then she did not want them. Australia it would be.

After more than a year in the detention camp, Mother, Khay, Mei, and Veng boarded an airplane and flew to their new land and life in Australia.

Houy had been sent to find Huor when he had failed to return from a buying trip to Thailand. She had left Phnom Penh in the company of our half sister Eng, whom she had met before she left the capital and who also wanted to leave the country. Father had been married to another Chinese born Cambodian woman, who had died years before he met Mother. Eng had never been very nice to us and her disposition had only worsened after the loss of her husband and children to the Khmer Rouge's purges. However, family was family, and they travelled together.

The two girls paid a people smuggler to get them across the border and into the refugee camps. Houy's journey was relatively uneventful, until the group they were travelling with was waylaid by a dozen armed bandits. They robbed the people, of course, but they were particularly taken by Houy, who was ethnic Chinese and had pale skin to go with it. Officially the men were disgusted by her appearance and went to great lengths to make their distaste clear. A protracted argument broke out to determine the order in which the men would rape Houy, but just as a consensus was reached another group of refugees were spied through the trees. The opportunity to add to their loot was too good to pass up and greed won out over lust. Honour among thieves being what it was, none of the bandits were willing to guard Houy, lest they miss out on their share of the spoils.

Houy ran for it the instant they left, and found a rice paddy close by. She hid by lying in the water with just her mouth and nose exposed to let her breathe, while the bandits searched the area for their intended victim. They eventually gave up and left for easier sport, but when Houy returned to the travelling group they would not let her rejoin them. They were afraid that she would attract further unwanted attention. One of the other men took it upon himself to guide her the rest of the way to the border, and she eventually met up with the rest of the group as they stole into the refugee camp.

Houy found no sign of our brother Huor amidst the press of refugees, and in the end she registered as an orphan. Her chances of finding one person in a foreign country had never been all that good in the first place, and so she just had to make the best of a bad situation. Shortly after their arrival Eng met an old friend who happened to have found her way to the same camp. Eng decided to leave Houy and go to live with her friend, who was somewhat better off. She said that her friend could not afford to help support them both, and that Houy would need to find somewhere else to live. So much for family.

Deciding to be bold, Houy went to the camp administrator and asked him if he wanted a maid. She had noticed that he had a small daughter and another baby due soon, by the look of his wife. The administrator agreed to the offer as long as Houy was willing to accept only food as payment, rather than money. Her job was to take care of their daughter, cook, wash clothes and do the housework. It was not a particularly generous offer but it was better than anything else that was available. People said that it looked like the administrator had acquired a second wife, although he was an honourable man if somewhat harried, and never took advantage of his position. For a time at the camp Houy enjoyed more and better food than Eng, and it began to seem as if there was something to that Karma business after all.

Eng found that she needed to work harder than she liked in order to maintain her welcome with her friend, and managed to persuade Houy that they would be better off sticking together. Even after all the depredations that she had been through, Houy still thought the best of people, especially when they were family. She quit her job, moved back in with her half sister and was immediately the poorer for it.

Houy made a friend who had been brought to the camp by her parents, who had the means to send her to the small school that existed within the wire. Each day Houy would walk with her to the dilapidated building that some of the more educated and enterprising refugees used to give lessons in Chinese. Houy would wait patiently outside as there was simply nothing else for her to do most of the time. After several months the teacher spied her, and asked the class who the silent girl sitting by the door was. She was told that Houy was an orphan who could not afford the tiny payment for classes. The teacher told Houy's friend to bring her inside and gave her free lessons for the rest of her time in the camp. It was a small kindness in a place where such gestures were both uncommon and profound in their effect.

In 1981 both Houy and Eng were chosen to go to the United States. As official orphans, they were sponsored by a church group that had taken pity on the plight of the Cambodian refugees. The church proved to be a powerful ally and unlike most other people, their paths to America were relatively smooth. Once in the United States they lived in Arizona for several months; however, Eng met a new boyfriend who lived in New York. Eng decided to move to New York to be with him, leaving Houy behind in Arizona. It was he who said no to this plan because Houy was only eighteen years old at that time, and it did not seem right to him to leave her behind alone. That summed up Eng's feelings towards the members of my family. Random strangers tended to treat Houy better than Eng ever did.

Houy moved to New York with them and attended school as well as working as a cleaner in a large office building at night. After six months in the United States the Thai embassy sent her a letter. It said that in two days her brother Khay would be leaving Thailand, bound for America to live with her. Houy was beside herself with excitement at the thought of Khay's arrival. He was such a dynamic personality that he could not help but make her life better in every way. Two days after the letter arrived, Houy received a phone call to tell her that Khay had vanished from the refugee camp, presumably gone back to Cambodia for some unfathomable reason.

Houy cried for days at the news, but then a month later the telephone rang with another message from the immigration authorities. Khay had reappeared in the camp, this time with his mother and the twins in tow. Then he had evaporated once more, only to return yet again with more people to whom he did not even seem to be related. The embassy fervently hoped that he would stay put this time. Houy restarted her sponsorship application over again and waited for the arrival of a large part of her family with growing excitement. Though she was very poor herself, she still managed to regularly send money to Mother in the refugee camp.

Before long, however, Houy was notified that Mother had decided to go to Australia instead of America. Houy was in two minds at this news. She was sad that there would be no reunion any time soon, but glad that at least some of her family were safe at last. Houy considered moving to Australia, but Mother told her that she was safe in a developed country and that she should stay there. Houy obeyed Mother's wishes—we all usually did.

- 21 -

Please Hold

After days aboard the boat, Father and I finally approached the shore at about midday. The captain had Father sign his proof of delivery document and we were left there on a rickety bamboo dock, squinting in the bright sunshine. We had spent the entire morning in the dim bilge and our eyes watered in the bright light. The boat immediately moved away and blended in among the dozens of other vessels by the shore. My first impression was that Australia looked disappointingly like the fishing village we had left in Cambodia. My second thought was that the armed policemen who were running towards us along the shore did not look like the 'round eyes' I had been led to expect. It finally dawned on me that we were not in Australia at all, but were instead in Thailand.

The policemen need not have hurried; after days squatting in the boat we could barely stand on the shaky dock, let alone run. They were shouting and running towards us but we did not understand a word of what they were saying. The policemen ran onto the dock, causing it to sway alarmingly, and came to a halt with their guns pointed right at us. One of them shouted what sounded like a question but we could not possibly answer. He tried again in a louder voice but eventually gave up and they prodded us towards their jeep at gunpoint. They drove us to a police station and tried different languages until they discovered that we understood Chinese. They interviewed Father at length about his background and plans for the future. We were certainly not the first such arrivals in the area and there were no great surprises to be learned from us.

They seemed to be satisfied with Father's answers, and given my young age they showed no interest in questioning me. We were taken back to the jeep, driven to a big stilt house and told via some pointed gestures and pantomimed threats to stay there. There were no fences or guards but we had no idea where we were. We did not know the language to ask directions and even if we had, we had no money to run away with. There was no one living in the house but it was locked up tight and so we slept on the concrete slab underneath the raised timber floor, listening to the wind howling through the trees. The wind was loud but I felt a sense of peace creeping over me as I lay there. Death had followed me like a shadow for so long that I had forgotten what it was like to relax. I had not heard a single gunshot since we left Cambodia, and I felt the resentment that we had not been brought to Australia leave me. For the first time in ten years I fell asleep feeling safe.

Other families had been brought to the house a few hours before us. None of us had any food or any way of getting some. The sea was close by, but we had no fishing equipment and no money. Even if we had, we did not know where a market might be and we could not ask. Two Thai soldiers came by in a jeep soon after we arrived and unceremoniously dumped onto the ground two fresh stingrays, a bag of rice, some salt and three pots. The stingray meat was not very tasty but we were grateful for anything we were given. I helped out with what cooking and cleaning there was to do, given that we were sleeping under a house and had little enough to eat.

Possibly because of the long and damp boat journey, I fell very ill. All I could do was lie on the ground with a fever burning through my body. I became dizzy whenever I tried to stand up, but I knew that I had to take care of myself if I was to look after Father. I staggered across to the occupied stilt house across the road and crawled up the stairs on my hands and knees. The owner of the house was Thai and did not speak any Khmer or Chinese, but he felt my forehead and the heat of my fever. I shut my eyes and tears started to run down my cheeks. Surely this should be how my own father should look after me, rather than sitting and wanting to be waited on, hand and foot. The man gave me four tablets and spoke some words that were presumably instructions, but I did not understand them. Pills are pills though, so I managed to swallow two before falling asleep on the ground under a tree. I woke a few hours later and took the remaining two pills. I was unable to help much around the camp for several days and went to bed each night with an empty stomach. That suited me because all I wanted to do was sleep. Either by luck or because the medicine worked, I recovered over the next few days.

Father and I were left to our own devices for a week or so. Then a large truck arrived and we were transported to the *Sikhiu* detention centre. As we entered I had a feeling of being reborn, free of fear and danger. I was in Thailand among other escapees and this place had been built for people who were on their way towards a new and better life. On arrival we were kept busy for several weeks, getting to know the routine and what went where. Father was subjected to more interviews and we had our photos taken for the record. He immediately wrote a letter to Mother so that she could begin the sponsorship process to reunite us all. Things were now beginning to look up and there was nothing to do now but wait. And wait.

Most of the people in the detention centre were Vietnamese refugees who had left their country by boat in the same way we had. There were only a few other Cambodian/Chinese families but at least we had some people to talk to. We were surrounded on all sides by barbed wire fences and we slept on the dirt floor of a shack that was about ten metres long and four wide. Each building held about thirty people and there were about fifty shacks inside the camp. We were not allowed to wander outside the fence and there were dire warnings against trying to escape. There was a separate fenced area inside the detention centre for those captured on the wrong side of the fence. Anyone breaking the rules risked arrest, and repeat offenders would have their heads forcefully shaved and be made to sit in the hot sun for days on end.

A loud wake up call was broadcast every morning at sunrise to rouse the refugees to do some exercise. The intention may have been good but the response was half hearted at best. Food was distributed on a weekly basis and it was hard not to compare this situation with the one the Khmer Rouge had enforced. Once a week we were each given one bucket of water, one hundred grams of fish, one cup of rice and two pieces of charcoal. Father and I were used to food being in short supply, but this was a starvation diet and there was nowhere we could go to find anything extra. I wished for the day when we would not have to carefully ration every morsel of food and every drop of water.

The administrators of the camp did not want the refugees to have any contact with the outside world. We were trouble enough just by being there and they plainly did not know what to do with so many desperate people. Some people within the camp had items to trade, such as gold that had not been spent on their journey or stolen on arrival. Thai merchants hovered outside the barbed wire like nervous flies. They ran to the fence when the patrolling soldiers were on the opposite side of the camp. They sold anything we could possibly want, provided we had the money. Refugees would make a rapid trade and blend back into the crowd before they could be caught and their goods confiscated. Father and I had no money or gold so I could only stare with envy at the people with their purchased food, medicine, soap and other luxuries.

Father had sent his letter to Mother weeks before and every morning we listened carefully to the announcements over the camp public address system, hoping for a message. Most of the words from the speakers were gibberish to us but we knew that Father would be called by name if a reply came from Mother. After several months we finally heard his name and he went to the office where a letter from Mother awaited. More importantly to our empty stomachs, she had sent some money at last. It was a money order transfer that could only be redeemed by Father and could not be stolen before it reached him.

We could now supplement our tiny food ration with instant noodles and other items from the Thai merchants that lined the other side of the barbed wire fence. Some of them must have struck a deal with the camp's administrators, presumably for some sort of payment. They were allowed to bring goods inside the camp and sold all sorts of biscuits, instant noodles and other delicious items. I longed to buy the sweets and biscuits that were on offer but I did not dare to spend one baht on unnecessary items. Father had given me a wad of money to buy food and I guarded it with my life. I would buy something like a packet of instant noodles and some *trokuon* water vegetables to make a pot of soup. That would be our meal for a typical day, but once a week we were able to buy more nutritious foods like chicken and pork.

Father never helped with cooking or fetching water. Even if he had been in better physical shape, he regarded domestic duties as female chores. I had been taking care of Father since Mother left Phnom Penh when I was fourteen years old. He was my responsibility and I had to cook for him, wash his clothes, and care for him as long as we were together. My days were spent wandering around the tiny world that was the camp, looking for cheap vegetables, firewood and water. I saw English classes being taught by Vietnamese refugees who had learned the language before leaving their country. I was well aware that I would need English skills if I ever left the camp and arrived in Australia. There was just no money to spare on education, and I began to feel my resentment towards Father grow. I felt that he should be helping more, regardless of his age, and that he should let go of the old ways and do a bit of 'women's work' when the situation called for it.

Over time we accumulated a few possessions. These consisted of two pairs of clothing each, a light towel, a straw mat that we slept on, a mosquito net that we slept under, two galvanised buckets for water, a cooking pot, two bowls, two spoons and a clay pot stove. The coal that the camp supplied did not go very far and we had to buy extra charcoal for cooking. I used our one pot to cook rice, which I then emptied into the bowls. After that I would reuse the pot to cook soup. The only consolation in having so few material goods was that washing up afterwards took no time at all.

The monsoon season came while we waited in the camp. It rained for hours each day, and for weeks at a time we could do nothing. Cooking had to be done under cover, with people taking turns to use whatever facilities were available. The rest of the time we just sat in our huts and waited it out. Conversation was almost impossible with what sounded like a minor waterfall hammering on the tin roof. The only break in the monotonous drone of the rain was the frequent and truly awesome cracks of thunder that followed each flash of nearby lightning. The grounds of the camp were a sea of mud but at least there was no flooding. The Thais were well experienced with monsoon weather and had created enough drainage to carry away the water.

Like I had just after landing in Thailand, Father also fell ill. He was convinced that he was going to die there in that refugee camp. In the quiet of the night he told me to go on to Australia alone. He said that the camp was as far as he could take me and that from there I would have to go on by myself. He said that I had been able to take care of him for so long that without him, I could look after myself. He said goodbye and then went to sleep. Curled on the ground in the corner of the hut, I started quietly crying, for although he was a shadow of his former self, he was still an adult figure for me to look up to. Father lived through the night and recovered over the next few days, but his health seemed to be on a downward spiral.

Looking back I think he was simply depressed. He could not see any future for himself and we had waited in the camp for so long. We had no idea how much longer we would have to rot in that dreary place, or even if we would ever leave. I do not know what happened to my father during the years of the Khmer Rouge's rule. As a former Chinese businessman, Father had probably lived through a nightmare even worse than my own. He would never speak of it, but it was plain that it had broken his spirit.

Inside the camp almost everyone else spoke Vietnamese and

I did not know one word of what they were saying. I hated feeling stupid as people around me chattered in their own language. All I heard was a series of sing-song sounds full of emotion but devoid of meaning. I had had enough and became friends with a Vietnamese girl who was staying in the same hut as Father and me. This was accomplished by smiles and hand gestures and there was little else to do, so at night after dinner we would sit together and she would teach me her language. She did not speak Khmer so the process was rather hit and miss, but I did soon begin to learn. We kept at it the entire time we were in the camp and after a year or so I was able to communicate in basic Vietnamese.

For a long time in the camp I had been preoccupied with the basics of survival. The relative peace I had first noticed after we arrived had masked the real situation and I began to notice the desperation around me. The camp had no work for the refugees. Water and food was trucked in, with a small amount grown in the limited area. Some food and luxuries could be bought, but whether you had money or not did not really matter. There was nothing to do and nowhere to go. It is impossible to describe the soul destroying effects of desperately wanting to leave a place and not knowing when, or even if, you would ever be allowed to do so.

My time in the camp felt like an eternity. Once a month there was a movie night that provided a short lived distraction, but the entertainment just showed us images of places we could not go to and foods that we could not afford to buy. Most people in jail know that there will come a time when they will go free, and they know with relative certainty when that will be. Leaving people in the limbo of a refugee camp is a slow torture, but it is a torture nonetheless. Some of the Vietnamese people had fled during their own war which had ended six years previously. They had squatted in the dust or occasionally the mud for six years, wondering whether they would ever be released. Six years of marking time, of existing but never really living. It could only end badly.

Protests were frequent and more or less ignored, unless they threatened to provoke an escape. The demonstrations took on their most extreme form when young men drenched themselves in petrol and set themselves on fire. Nothing I can write could begin to convey the desperation that would force a person to commit such an act. The United Nations High Commission for Refugees gave priority to people who had relatives in another country, particularly spouses or children. Father and I were lucky that we had both, and that Mother was already in Australia and could act as a sponsor for us. Our processing was far more rapid than that of many of the families around us. We waited a year and a half.

At long last, our names appeared on the list of families that were to be relocated to a transit camp called Phanat Nikom. There we would be given lessons about the Australian way of life and how to fit into our new country. I was full of excitement as it finally seemed that we would be going to a land of opportunity, peace and hope. Mother's letters had talked about the fact that the Australian government actually gave people money for no other reason than that they needed it. I had never heard of such a thing and it certainly did not happen in Cambodia. I assumed that she was joking.

We were taken by truck to the new camp where we underwent further processing, health checks and paperwork. We were told that Australia had accepted us as refugees and that we would be taken to the same city as Mother and my siblings. The official that was filling in the various forms asked me what my birth date was, which rather put me on the spot since I had no idea of the answer. After a moment of frantic thought, I said that it was the first of the first. I chose that date because it was easy to remember and who knew? At least some of it might have even been correct.

The new camp was much the same as the last. There were large huts shared by many people with nothing to do but sit and wait for their applications for immigration to be accepted by a third country. We still received food and water rations and they were still not enough, but we were not about to complain. Soon we would embark on the final stage of a long and painful journey that had shattered our nation and which had lasted for more than half of my life. Compared to the time that we had already waited in the previous refugee camp, the transit centre was a model of speed and efficiency. We only stayed there for three months.

For many of the people in Phanat Nikom there was no hope. Father and I had been brought there as part of some unfathomable bureaucratic process that presumably had a purpose. Others had been dumped there as soon as they arrived in Thailand. Some would never get a chance to experience freedom.

Once again our names appeared on the notice board and we had three days to pack and get ready. I asked why we were given three days to prepare. We had virtually nothing to take with us and I really only needed three minutes. We had been told that meals and beds would be provided at our destination, so I arranged to give all our cooking and sleeping equipment to a widow and her three children. The clothes Father and I wore were typical for refugees, but we were told that they were not good enough for Australia. We spent the very last of our money buying one outfit each that would hopefully fit into the Western way of life. We were sent to yet another camp called the Suan Plu Detention Centre in

Bangkok. Father and I were well used to the drill by now and settled down yet again to wait. This time it was for only three weeks.

At first the airport seemed scary. I had never lived in a world where there was advanced technology and I had never seen an aircraft up close before. I looked at the huge thing and wondered if it could really fly like a bird. I searched to see where the bombs came from until Father told me that this plane did not carry weapons. I rapidly got over my fear and finally knew that we were really leaving now and that the plane would carry us far away from the misery of the refugee camps. I boarded the plane wearing my new clothes and clutching every possession I owned. I carried a small folding umbrella.

Father and I sat back in the soft seats and listened to the unfamiliar noises as the doors were sealed. The sound from the engines built into a roar unlike anything I had ever heard before and I thought something must have gone wrong. Suddenly we surged down the runway and into the air, which made me feel like I had left my stomach behind. I relished the feeling as it meant we were on our way to Australia at last. I suddenly realised that Mei's premonition all those years before had now become my reality. I was in her plane heading to a safe and wonderful new life. I was on my way to education, opportunity, technology and freedom.

Excitement soon turned to boredom because Father and I had very little to do on the airplane. Before take-off the hostesses had run through what I assumed was a safety demonstration, but we were not much the wiser for it. The announcements were in English but at least we were able to figure out how to put on our seat belts. We were in the middle aisle so I could not see out of the small windows. I would have liked to look outside but I had never in my life been in such an artificial environment, and it seemed safest to stay in my seat. There were magazines in the pockets on the back of the seat in front of me but I did not know if I was allowed to look at them or if I would be charged money if I did.

After we had been in the air for a while the noise from the engines dropped and the aircraft levelled out. We were offered food but it was completely unfamiliar to me and smelt very odd. I could not bring myself to eat the offering and wished I could just ask for some rice. As it happened, I had learned the words for one Western food item and so I tried my luck with that. The words were '*orange juice*' and soon the hostess brought me a glass of orange liquid. It was not very nice and I would have preferred plain water but I did not know how to ask.

Eventually I got up the nerve to follow another passenger to the back of the plane and discovered that there were toilets on board. I was pleased because I thought I would find water there and could finally get a drink. I locked myself in the tiny room and stared at the fittings in dismay. Not only was I unable to figure out how to get water from the sink, but the toilet itself was completely dry! I thought it was broken and waited for another cubicle to become vacant. The toilet bowl in that one was also devoid of water and I gave up. I returned to my seat, drank the juice and asked for more. The stewardesses must have really thought I loved orange juice by the time I asked for my fifth glass.

My excitement grew as the plane began to descend. It seemed to take an awfully long time, and I thought that we must have been flying hundreds of feet in the air. I was eager to see my new country and was thoroughly sick of orange juice by then. There was a bump and we were down. Australia at last!

Father and I walked off the plane into the terminal and I thought that there had been some horrible mistake: there were Asian people everywhere! I asked Father if we were about to be thrown into yet another refugee camp but then we were approached by a man who spoke Chinese. He told us that we were in Singapore and that we had to wait for another plane that would take us to Australia. He was an interpreter who was employed to guide people in our situation to the right terminal gate. We were told to wait and he would return before the flight boarded.

It was six hours before our flight boarded and I wandered around the terminal, staring at the shops in awe. There was an incredible amount of wealth on display behind the glass and I was particularly taken by a case that held Rado watches. I had never been granted my wish to own a watch, and these were the most beautiful and elegant examples I had ever seen. They did not seem to be that expensive either, judging by the small number of digits on the price tag. It turned out that I had not taken into account that the exchange rate between the Cambodian Riel and Singapore dollar was about three thousand to one. It did not matter either way; Father and I had precisely no money between us. After the unpalatable food on the flight, the rice and noodle dishes on sale at the airport restaurants were especially enticing. Nothing was free though, so we would just have to go hungry for a while longer.

Eventually the interpreter returned and showed us to the gate and we repeated the boarding and take-off procedures. The flight was longer and the aircraft was slightly different but the food was the same, as was the orange juice. If nothing else, the refugee camps had taught Father and me patience and we sat without complaint. Eventually the plane began to descend. A voice spoke over the public address system and I did not understand any of it except for one word: Australia.

The plane touched down and rolled to a halt at the gate. Father and I made our way into the terminal and finally I saw what I had longed for: hundreds and hundreds of Caucasian faces. I knew then that the killing fields were far behind me and I would never, ever, have to return.

No more waiting. No more death. No more war for me.

- 22 -

Australia

Father and I arrived in Adelaide, South Australia, in the autumn of 1985. As in Singapore, we were met by an interpreter who guided us through Customs and out of the airport. Of course we had no luggage to retrieve. The short walk from the terminal to the small bus was the coldest temperature I had ever experienced in my life, and I wondered if it was always this way in Australia. We joined a few other refugees in the vehicle but we did not speak their language and I never found out where they came from.

On the ride I stared out the window at my new country. It was different in every way from Cambodia. Everything was very neat and tidy. The roads were very smooth and clean, and the traffic was organised. None of the cars seemed to have horns. After the constant cacophony of traffic noise in Asia, I liked the quiet very much. I saw no food stalls on the roadside and when we stopped for any reason, no one tried to sell us anything at all. There were lots of cars, very few motorbikes and no animals whatsoever on the roads. For most of my life these proportions had been the exact opposite.

Houses were widely separated instead of being closely packed together and they were mostly only one storey tall rather than two or three. To make up for their lack of height, they were very wide and had very large gardens. Strangely though, the gardens rarely contained fruit trees or vegetable patches. It was almost as if the gardens were there just to look nice. Surely not, I thought, the edible plants must just look different here. The fences, if there were any, were low pickets that would not keep out even the laziest thief. In Phnom Penh the fences had sharp spikes or broken glass to prevent intrusion.

I thought that we would be taken straight to meet Mother and that we would be together again at last. Instead we were driven from the airport to the Pennington Detention Centre in North Adelaide. It was more like a hostel than any of the detention centres Father and I had been used to. It was, in fact, rather like the house we stayed under on first arriving in Thailand. We were not locked in and were free to wander around outside, but we did not know where we were and did not speak English. Father had Mother's address but did not know how to get there. The people at the detention centre were only there to feed us and keep things running. They were not there to help reunite lost families.

Our meals were prepared and served by a Caucasian lady and the food was once again completely alien to us. The lady gave us a ladle of each item on hand, and I just took whatever she gave me. I found it difficult to stomach the smell, let alone the tastes and textures. All I wanted was some plain rice and soy sauce but there was none on offer, so I picked at my plate and ate what I could. I do not mean to sound ungrateful because I am sure that the cooks were doing their very best and thought that they were serving us delicious food.

I had spent a long time hungry in Cambodia and there were times I had eaten anything and everything that I could. I wondered if the food of Cambodia would be as unpalatable for an Australian as the hostel food was for us. Would a starving Australian be able to eat a plate of rice topped with *prahoc*? The word translates to 'stinky fish' and was an apt description of a food that consists of small salted fish that had been pounded to bits and then fermented into a grey paste. To the uninitiated, it looked and smelled appallingly like rotten fish. The smell could make even a Khmer native wince when in its raw form, but it is considered a delicacy. I doubt very much that the average Westerner would touch it.

The centre had shared bathrooms and toilets and I was fascinated by the availability of hot and cold running water. I only needed to turn the tap on and out would pour a seemingly limitless supply of pure water. It never slowed to a dribble or stopped at all, so there was no need for a storage tub. I did not have to fetch water from a river or well that would be used up all too soon. I did not have to gather firewood and light a fire to boil water for drinking or washing. The toilets flushed at the pull of a chain or the push of a button, instead of having to dip a scoop of water from the trough. I had a difficult time with the toilets though because I had never used a toilet with a seat before. We had always had squat toilets or simply a hole in the ground. I could not imagine how to squat on such a thin rim and fell off several times. I did not know how Father managed.

Father and I knew that Mother, Khay, Mei and Veng were living somewhere in South Australia, which we assumed meant that they were not far away. We did not know at the time that South Australia was considerably larger than all of Cambodia. Five and a half times as large in fact. We stayed put at the detention centre until some weeks later, when a Chinese family came to visit in an attempt to recruit congregation members. Father went with them to the church and showed them Mother's address. It was less than five kilometres away.

The church family drove Father back to the centre to pick me up and fifteen minutes later we were outside a house in the suburbs. We waited by the road while our new friends went to the front door to make sure they had the correct address. Mother opened the door and after a few words spied us on the lawn. She ran out towards us and I was wrapped in a hug that had been four years in the making. Khay emerged from the house to see what the commotion was and joined in the celebration. There were a lot of tears shed over the course of the next few hours. Mother had been aware that we were on our way, but had no idea that we had been in Australia for several weeks. It did not matter. We were together again and safe.

We caught up on what had happened to everyone since we last saw each other, and it rapidly became apparent that no one had had an easy time of it. Everyone had felt the same sense of relief when the airplane they had travelled on had left the ground. Everyone had experienced the same sort of confusion when confronted with unfamiliar concepts and attitudes. Mother, Khay, Veng and Mei had managed to get a meal while in the air, but when they finished the odd tasting food, they found that they had a small wrapped square left over. They had said 'yes' to everything that even looked like it was being offered, but it never occurred to them to spread the substance on their bread roll. Khay had declared that he knew what it was for, and once they finished their butter flavoured coffee the three children concluded that white people had strange taste.

Mother dispensed some knowledge that was particularly relevant, especially for recent arrivals with little to no English. In Cambodia, we had grown up with a brand of packaged food products that was well known for its high quality. The company logo was a cat's head, and more than one family had assumed that the same was true in Australia. It turned out that the hundreds of cans in the supermarket isles bearing pictures of felines were in fact food for cats. Mother had no idea why it was apparently necessary to go to such trouble for animals that were perfectly capable of finding their own food.

Mother was renting a three-bedroom house that was almost devoid of furniture. I was surprised and pleased that we had a TV, even though I did not understand anything the people on the screen said. Apart from the TV set the house looked pretty bare, except for some mattresses on the floor in the bedrooms that had been donated by the church group. After sleeping for so long on either dirt or a bamboo mat on the dirt, the old mattresses were very comfortable to me. Over time we bought some furniture and clothes from St Vincent De Paul and the Salvation Army stores, but there was very little we had that was new.

Now that I was in Australia with my family and in a secure home, I next wanted an education. I began to think about going to university and becoming an Australian citizen. Before any of that could happen though, I needed to be able to communicate. Khay enrolled me in an English class and I joined a dozen or so Vietnamese students. The class ran for three months at a special school in North Adelaide and we studied only English. The majority of students had all attended school back in their home countries and some had actually finished high school. Not only was their English much better than mine, but they had done mathematics and science and could reel off the table of elements to prove it. I felt stupid among them but it made me more determined than ever to educate myself.

I did my very best, but no amount of classes or textbooks could ever prepare me for the idioms and slang expressions that the average Australian used without even thinking. A major obstacle was sarcasm, with all of its variations—some more subtle than others. Australians often use exaggeration or understatement, or say the opposite to what they really mean on the assumption that the listener will understand. 'Mmmn, nice dress' could mean exactly what the words expressed or just the opposite, depending upon the speaker's inflection. The fine details just had to wait. After three months I had the basics, but still had to listen very carefully and easily became lost if someone spoke too quickly.

Going to English class became like a hunger. Every night I anxiously looked forward to returning the next morning and every afternoon I studied diligently. As soon as I got home I had to help Mother cook dinner and afterwards I would go over my notes until bedtime. When I came to Australia I was almost eleven years behind my fellow students and though I could not catch up overnight, I did my best to narrow the gap as quickly as I could. I was dimly aware that many children did not enjoy school and actively tried to avoid it, but this seemed absurd to me. Under any normal circumstances, most Cambodian parents would demand that their children be educated as a means to finding a job and achieving financial security.

The bus journey to my classes was a difficult adventure at first. I could not ask for help and although I was told the bus number I was supposed to take, there were so many things I did not know. For one thing, I did not know how to make the bus stop where I needed it to. I had been raised with the manners of a good Cambodian girl, and it was considered impolite to look directly into the eyes of someone you were talking to, especially when speaking to an elder. To be safe I kept my head and eyes down most of the time, which meant that I never saw other passengers pull the cord to signal the driver to stop. I could hear the bell and I noticed that the bus stopped soon after, but by the time I looked up at the sound, it was too late to see what caused it.

I sat there on the bus as we passed by the school and panicked silently until some other people got off several stops later. I followed them off the bus and had to walk two kilometres back to my class. On the way home, the bus just happened to stop where I needed, so I still did not know the secret. The next day I made sure I kept my head up the whole trip and saw a lady ahead of me pull the cord to ring the bell. I never had to get off at the wrong stop again.

I was on the way to school one day when a group of Australian girls boarded the bus and sat in the row behind me. The bus was half empty and one of the girls started to pull on my hair. I turned around and looked at her but I did not know how to tell her to stop and she kept on doing it all the way to my stop. I was not willing to meekly leave the bus and pretend nothing had happened. Instead, I pulled the cord and as the bus was slowing to a stop I stood up, stomped on her foot as hard as I could and ran for the door. A bunch of bitchy teenagers were far less intimidating than land mines and Khmer Rouge soldiers.

One day our teacher was ill so our school principal acted as a substitute teacher. Rather than follow the usual curriculum, she brought a packet of coloured pencils to class and held them up one at a time, pronouncing the colour of each in English. When she had finished she started to go through each again, but this time she pointed to each of us in turn to say the colour out loud. When she called on me I found that I was not able to pronounce the word in English. I was so angry with myself that I went home and badgered Khay until I had the right pronunciation. I wrote them down phonetically in Khmer, although this proved difficult because some of the sounds used in English are simply not used in many Asian languages. There were no excuses though and I was determined to study hard no matter what obstacles were placed in front of me.

Even though we were in Australia and I was attending school, it was difficult to let go of the instincts that had kept me alive through my childhood. I was surprised to see that the local bird life was so tame that they more or less ignored people altogether. If you walked towards a bird it would stroll aside as if it had all the time in the world. Such behaviour in Cambodia would quickly land the creature in a cooking pot. I was on my way home from school when I saw a flock of fat wood ducks by a small pond near our house. I went home and took Khay back to see the silly birds. We decided to try catching one.

What followed was a feathered version of the chase that had ended in a meal of rat soup. I think the ducks could not quite believe what was happening and just kept waddling away from us, rather than taking flight to safety. After much pursuit and even more quacking, we caught one and I stuffed the bewildered creature into my school bag. I did not know that urban hunting was illegal and that we would be fined if we were caught. The duck was dispatched and cooked that night, but the meat was so gamey and tough that it was almost inedible. A grain fattened field rat was much to be preferred and it was probably for the best that the ducks were not palatable. If they had been, we would have immediately set to catching all we could and inevitably landed in trouble with the local authorities. Probably sooner rather than later.

I started high school at the beginning of the third term, which put me almost eleven years behind the other students. I was eighteen years old, with no real education and only the barest grasp of the English language. The lessons I had attended in Phnom Penh had been long ago, short lived and very different from the Australian curriculum. No doubt if there had been a class on jungle survival I would have been in my element. As it was, I was lost in classrooms where only English was spoken. I was unable to understand the chatter, the manners, the fads and fashions of my peers. At home my parents understood even less and were unable to help me with either homework or my social adjustment. Parent-teacher nights were a lesson in futility.

My appearance presented some problems that were embarrassing rather than merely matters of practicality. We had come to Australia with nothing and most of our clothes were donated by the church group. They were not cut for an Asian frame and we were very skinny, especially when we first arrived. My pants did not fit and the belt I wore was only tenuously able to stay in place. I not only looked different because of my heritage, but I also dressed strangely and could barely communicate. These were three strikes that added up to the social kiss of death. Fortunately I did not care one bit because I had other concerns. Other cultural differences were harder to ignore than the fashions of the day.

Cambodian culture honours age and it is a compliment to mention the advanced years of someone because it means that they are wise and worthy of respect. In reality they may be a blithering idiot, but an aged person is assumed to have superior knowledge. The young do not point out the shortcomings of their elders, no matter how obvious. The Australian emphasis is often on youth, the drive to be fit, to have a firm body and an unlined face. It is in direct opposition to the respect paid to the aged in the

Cambodian culture, where there is simply no equivalent phrase to 'silly old bugger'. In Khmer, these words would be a contradiction in terms.

Many Cambodian people find it attractive when people have pale skin and look like they have plenty of food to eat. Being skinny means one is probably poor, and to be mildly overweight is seen as a sign of prosperity. An Asian person calling someone else 'fat' may not be saying it as an insult and could mean simply that they are tall or muscular. Of course they may also mean that the person is in fact plump, but in either case they are probably paying a compliment. A tanned skin signals to a Cambodian that one works outdoors, probably in a menial job. To the average Australian it means that someone has a lot of leisure time or has been on holiday.

The relationship between children and adults was another area in which cultural differences ran deep. In my family the children did not speak in the presence of adults unless invited to do so. We were expected to be disciplined, quiet and respectful. When parents made family decisions they did not invite the opinions of their children. Khay was somewhat of an exception to this rule, but even he would do as he was told if Mother or Father really put their foot down.

Direct communication was difficult for recently arrived Cambodian people. Every issue was skirted around, and if someone became upset they would never just come out and say so. The injured party would complain to everyone they knew and eventually the other might come to hear of it, but it always seemed a very inefficient method to me. I thought that Cambodians internalised their emotions more than was good for them as we dealt with the enormous pain of our history in silence. The flow-on effect of this has affected every part of our culture to the point where we just do not express ourselves with words. There may be plenty of talk, but often nothing of substance is said. I have never heard my father or mother say that they loved me.

Communication with people from my own culture was easy though, compared to my bewilderment of English in general and Australian slang in particular. I was at a function of some sort and a woman asked me, 'You're not hungry, are you?' I had just eaten so I replied yes, meaning that I was indeed not hungry. I was promptly handed a plate of food, which I ate so as not to give offence and so that it did not go into the bin. I had seen people waste huge amounts of food in Adelaide, and I knew that there were hungry people still in the refugee camps. I could not bring myself to throw away anything edible.

The differences between the land of my birth and the land I found myself in could all be ignored in the classroom. I loved school even if I had to study both the subject matter and the language at the same time. I always sat in the front row whenever I could and listened intently to every word the teacher spoke. For the first time in my life I was receiving a comprehensive education and I did not even have to pay for the privilege. I had never even heard of free education before I came to Australia, and I saw it as a ticket out of poverty that had to be grabbed with both hands in case it slipped away. Mother always reminded us that no matter what people may steal from us, they would never be able to take away our knowledge. For the life of me, I could not understand why some of the other students seemed disinterested in studying. I asked one why she came to school if she did not want to learn and she replied that she had to. I did not understand her answer.

A year after arriving in Australia Father was deeply depressed and became ill. He had not learned to speak any English and it would have been almost impossible for him to do so at his age even if he had tried his best. He was able to socialise once a week with the people at church, but only if one of the congregation was able to drive him there. Since we had arrived he had been house bound, with none of the social networks he would have had in Cambodia. In Asia it was never far to a temple, market or town square where the elderly would gather every day to discuss everything from politics to the weather or the achievements of their children. In Adelaide, everything was much farther apart and so Father had nowhere to go, and there was virtually nothing for him to do to fill his day.

Mother rented Chinese language video tapes from an Asian supermarket for Father to watch. These were lengthy and incredibly slow-paced operas which would have made the most placid local version seem action packed in comparison. Father would have breakfast in the morning and be watching the videos as we left for school. When we returned he would still be there, staring at the screen and often crying quietly to himself. I never found out whether his tears were because the story was sad, or if he was simply pondering what his life had become.

Father's health had declined rapidly since arriving in Australia, with high blood pressure on top of numerous other problems. One day he stubbed his toe which became so swollen and bruised that he was unable to walk. His legs also swelled up to the point where he became bedridden. He ended up at the Royal Adelaide Hospital and I went to visit him after school every day. One day he told me that he was having many visitors, and named them one after the other. I mentioned this to Mother and she told me that all of Father's 'visitors' were people long since dead.

Father could no longer eat solids, so I brought him some tins of his favourite fruits like lychees and longans. I spoon fed him the juice from the cans and packed up the solid fruit to take back home so that it was not wasted. As I was leaving for the night, Father grabbed hold of my hand and said that he did not want me to go. I had to go to school the next day and still had study to do that night, so I told him that I would see him again the next day. My fingers slipped from his as he slowly loosened his grip, and I left him lying there. I did not know that it would be the last time I would see my father alive. He died alone that night, a year after arriving in Australia.

My father was buried at Hindmarsh Cemetery in the spring of 1986. The Chinese members of his church attended and donated a big bunch of flowers to put on top of his coffin. I did not cry at the funeral. If pressed for a reason, I would guess that for a long time my father had not acted as a father to me. I had always expected him to be a strong figure, to provide for and protect his family. Since we had left Kratie for the final time, I had not seen Father as the head of the family. Mother had driven us onwards, out of the countryside to the city and then out of Cambodia altogether. Even before then, he had been weak and so slow that we had to hire transport for him to ride to escape the artillery that was falling around us. With a child's eyes I had seen him as old and useless. I was wrong. He had done the best that he could, for as long as he could, and later I did cry for him. He was my father and I loved him.

A movie called *The Killing Fields* was released while I was in high school. I found that some of my classmates had heard of it and became interested in my background and where I had come from. I found myself explaining that Cambodia was indeed a real country, though much smaller than Australia. Most of the other children had never heard of it, and only knew of Asian countries that were unavoidably large, such as China and India. Vietnam was an exception because Australia had been involved in its war, and it had been well publicised. By contrast, the upheaval inflicted upon Cambodia had been carried out at first in secret and afterwards was ignored by the rest of the world for a long time.

Some of the other students had seen the movie and wondered if any real life experience could actually be that ghastly. The movie was a starting point, one that I could use to explain things to people if they asked. I told as best I could what it was like to live in Cambodia during the years of Khmer Rouge reign. At the time, I did not have the words to tell the story properly. I could say that real events had been far worse than any film could possibly portray, but I could not make them feel it. I could not make them see the eight-year-old girl who was murdered right before me, the smell of her blood, or the hideous stink of a month old mass grave. I could not take them to those dark places that echoed with the screams of the dying and the wails of mothers as their children were torn from their arms. I could not show them what it was really like, and in truth I did not really try. No one should ever have to witness such depravity. If I could somehow make them see they would have hated me forever, and they would have been right to. They would never have recovered from the experience. I never have.

When in the classroom I tried to sit in the front row so that I could concentrate on the lesson without disruption. The students that were not interested in studying sat at the back of the class and rarely paid attention to the teacher. I often thought that they could do with a dose of Cambodian discipline, which usually involved a long cane and high velocity. If a student saw their teacher outside of school on the streets of Phnom Penh, they would bow as a sign of respect and say *chumriap sua,* which is a respectful greeting reserved for people that one honours the most. School for me was all business, and I never had the money to pay for excursions, formals, class photos, or any other activity with an associated cost.

Even though I was attending classes full-time, I still needed to work to help support my family. None of us could get well, or even moderately paid jobs. A lack of education and English skills meant that we were unable to do anything but the most menial work. Veng and I found jobs after school as cleaners in the State Bank of South Australia. I was well aware of the low status of my task and at the time the concept of 'face', of personal honour and pride, was still vital to me. I hated the idea of having to work in a menial position, when so many better jobs existed for those with the right skills. At least the work was easy, particularly for some-one used to the long hours of manual labour we had been forced to endure under the watchful eyes of the Khmer Rouge.

As soon as I could, I began to learn to drive so that our family would be less reliant on the public transportation system. I sat the written test for my learner permit after memorising the booklet provided by the traffic authority over the course of a week. Khay began to teach me how to drive, once again acting as a father fig-ure, and doing so in more ways than one. Asian teachers and par-ents can be impatient when educating their children and Khay was no exception. He had obtained his licence soon after arriving in Australia and had at least two years' practice. He immediately forgot the fact that he had once had to learn to drive from scratch, and was impatient with my fumbling efforts. I think that he would have preferred to short-cut the whole learning process by pushing me and the car down a large hill. Khay also taught me how to read a road directory, although he again used something of a sink or swim method. He would point to a random place on the map and say 'Go there!' After eight lessons with Khay, passing the practical driving test was no trouble at all.

Mother had bought an old Ford Fairlane that was a muddy brown colour so unappealing, that it was a wonder she had to buy it at all. The idea was that during school holidays I would drive Veng, Mei and as many other people as could legally fit into the car to pick fruit at the farms in the Adelaide hills. Non-family passengers paid five dollars for the journey. The road to the farms was long, winding, and often had a cliff face on one side and a deep valley on the other. Mother did not know that the route was challenging for a beginning driver, and it was probably more by good luck than good management that we made those first few journeys without incident. Mother would rise each day at 5am to cook our lunch and we would leave home at six.

Years of struggling to find every edible or useful scrap had prepared us well to be fruit pickers. We were fast and thorough, climbing to the top of the cherry trees and stripping them clean from top to the bottom. Some of the other workers only picked around the bottom of the trees where they could easily reach, leaving the fruit at the top for the birds. The farm owner did not like that at all, and called us back year after year. We were paid according to the amount of fruit we picked and so we never stopped to take our lunch break. We worked through each day, only stopping for fifteen minutes in the morning and afternoon. We were exhausted at the end of each day, not getting home until at least six p.m. The farm experience was a spur to me. I did not want to pick fruit for the rest of my life and I knew what I had to do to avoid that fate.

There were no excuses for failure. Here in Australia I would not be able to say that my opportunities were limited. This was a land of opportunity, education and freedom and I had only to take my chance. During lunch breaks I sought out my teachers for assistance with any classes I was having difficulties with. In truth that was most of them, because I really was a terribly long way behind. My teachers did not mind me badgering them at every opportunity and they would often shorten their lunch hour to answer my endless questions. I think that they were delighted by any student who truly wanted to learn, and they spent hours with me every week. I knew that I would not get any help at home and we could not afford a tutor, so I continued to dog my teachers' heels for the entire time I was at school. School was paradise; free education, no war, and no corruption. I became an Australian citizen in my final year of high school. I was told that now no one could ever make me leave.

Despite the difficulties we faced, I did well at school. Most of the Cambodian girls in my year spoke better English than I did, but they were not very interested in study. They wanted only to be popular and spent most of their time trying to attract the attention of the boys. They went so far as to bring multiple changes of clothes, makeup and jewellery to school every day. The better they looked the worse their marks became, and some were married by the end of Year Ten. Most of the rest had left school during Year Eleven and very few indeed completed Year Twelve. Only two girls from Cambodia went on to university that year: my sister Mei and me.

My education was the most important thing to me, but Mother did not allow homework to interfere with my daily chores. She thought that a study desk was an extravagance and I had to make do with what little furniture we already had in our house. Our landlord was an Italian man who came to inspect the house every month. He would run his finger across the windowsills, checking for dust, as if it made a difference to him. Mother did not want to give a bad impression and made us hand clean all the windows every weekend, inside and out. The experience made me want more than ever to own my own house. I promised myself that as soon as I started earning real money, I would buy my own home where no one could tell me what to do.

I would stay for hours at the university library to study and escape the endless housework that Mother made us do. She insisted that we get an education but it did not seem to register with her that she had become our major obstacle.

Once a week, Mother bought off-cuts of meat from a local butcher for about fifty cents per kilogram. Other people used the bony stuff for pet meat, but we turned it into soup and wasted nothing. Mother travelled to the central markets every Sunday to buy cheap vegetables, fruits and chicken bones to extend our money as far as possible. We could not walk past a fruit-bearing tree without stripping it, if we possibly could. We were no longer in the dire straits that we had been in Cambodia; indeed we were by then relatively wealthy compared to many that we had left behind. It was impossible to forget the gnawing hunger though, and our automatic reaction was to get the most out of every single dollar. We never went out just for fun or paid for a meal in the entire time I lived in Adelaide.

Mother grew Asian greens and herbs in the backyard, and we had to help pick, wash and tie them into neat bunches. We spent hours early each morning in preparation, and then I had to drop off the completed bunches at a local Asian shop before making my way to university. We received the princely sum of twenty cents for each bunch of coriander and forty cents for the greens, but only payable in goods from the store, not as cash. Anything that was not sold was at our expense and I thought the whole enterprise was not worth the effort. In Cambodia a few extra dollars a day would make a huge difference, but in Australia it amounted to very little. I might not have minded so much if I could have just used some of that hard earned money for an occasional can of orange soda or a custard tart. I had a craving for sugar that would desert me long before I had money of my own and was able to indulge myself. It was a peculiar fact that our family operated much like a tiny communist country even though we had gone to great, not to mention dangerous, lengths to escape just that possibility. Needless to say, the routine of work and study left precious little time for friends, fun or recreation.

My final grades in Year Twelve had been good enough to enter a Computer Science degree at Flinders University. Language was still a problem, but I excelled at anything involving numbers. Computer languages are new to everyone when they first see them, so English skills were less of a problem. There is very little to tell about my university experience that was different from high school. I kept to myself, studied hard and generally stalked my lecturers for assistance at every opportunity.

I graduated with a Bachelor's Degree in Computing at the end of 1990, and started work at the beginning of 1991 as an Information Technology Officer in a Commonwealth government department in Canberra. Remembering fussy landlords, I bought my first house two months later. No one could come uninvited to inspect my housekeeping anymore; for the first time in my life no one could tell me what to do. I was free.

When I escaped Cambodia in 1983 I never intended to

return—there were far too many ghosts waiting for me. By 2005, however, I had finally healed enough to return to the land of my birth. I did not visit the killing fields or the Tuol Sleng Museum that had hosted the death of so many. I had witnessed the horror firsthand and did not need the lesson on the inhumanity of man, so I left the museum and its grisly exhibits to the tourists. I suppose they wandered through the old brick buildings, subdued into whispers by the weight of what they were seeing and thinking themselves lucky that nothing like this could happen where they came from. They were wrong of course, just lucky that a person with the right combination of charisma and madness had never come to power in their country. Cambodia has changed a lot over the years; everyone is concerned only with making a living and the children are untouched by the country's bloody history. They are often completely unaware of the events that I remember so keenly.

I visited Kratie and found the house I was born in and lived for that brief happy period. The current owners now sell gold from the shop on the ground floor. My father had built well, the house is still in good condition. The dolphins still frolic in the river nearby; their home was never taken from them.

Life has to be lived for it to be worthwhile, and once I was in my mid thirties I had the time and resources to do many things that I couldn't in the past. I had lost so much of my childhood that I wanted to make up for at least part of it. Far from the hot and humid jungles of my homeland, I now travel, snow ski, practise Taekwondo, hike, ride, rollerblade and generally answer to no one. I volunteer at the local Red Cross providing food to the less fortunate; I can never forget what it feels like to be hungry. I still live in Canberra with my beautiful daughter, who has completed two Bachelor's degrees and is now studying towards a PhD in Psychology. Other than her birth, nothing terribly momentous has happened for the last twenty years.

I like it that way.

Epilogue

My eldest sister Keang tried to escape from Cambodia on several occasions, but increased border security and the fact that she had three young children made such attempts expensive, dangerous and ultimately futile. She resigned herself to staying where she was and in 1980 married her husband Peng. They and their three children lived with her in-laws in Phnom Penh until 1994, at which time Mother managed to sponsor her immigration to Australia as part of the family reunion program. Keang was fortunate in that she was able to avoid the slow suffocation of the refugee camps. My sister and her family now live in their own home in Adelaide, only a kilometre from Mother's house. She has since had a fourth child and works in a retirement village caring for the elderly.

My eldest brother Huor also remained in Cambodia and was married in Phnom Penh in 1981. Sadly, his wife died soon after the birth of their third child. He remarried in 1993 and fathered two more sons. Mother tried unsuccessfully for eighteen years to sponsor him to Australia, under the same reunion program that had accepted Keang. He was finally able to immigrate to Australia in 2005 after Veng provided a sponsor guarantee. This means that if needed, Veng will financially support Huor, his wife and his children for the first ten years of their new life. Huor and his family now live in Adelaide with Mother, where he looks after her day-to-day needs as she becomes increasingly frail with age.

My elder sister Houy remained alone in America until she realised that there would not be the family reunion she had always hoped for. She married in 1984 and remains in New York to this day. Houy gained an Associate Degree in Finance and works at a major bank. She and her husband own several properties and are considering immigrating to be closer to her family. Houy has three children and eventually got her reunion, although not under the circumstances she would have liked. She visited all of her family in Australia after Father passed away.

My youngest sister Mei moved from Adelaide to Sydney in 1991, after completing a Bachelor in Computing. Despite initially entering the information technology field, she eventually returned to university for a career change to nursing in 2008. It was always a field that had appealed to her more than the sterile world of computing, and she excelled in her new studies. She is now a registered psychiatric and medical nurse, and lives in her own home in Sydney, with her partner and their two children.

Her twin Veng also completed a Bachelor in Computing in 1992 and was a system administrator for a while, but he never found the work satisfying. Like his twin Mei, he found himself in Sydney where he worked in a variety of jobs, before becoming a police officer with the New South Wales Police Force in 2002. He owns two properties and married in 2003. He now has two sons, who keep him on his toes more than the criminals of Sydney ever did.

My elder brother Khay completed a diploma as an interpreter/translator as well as a diploma in Mechanical Engineering. He worked for a number of government departments in Australia as an interpreter for three major Chinese dialects, as well as Khmer. He married in 1990 and has two sons. In 2002 he saw the potential for the economy of Cambodia to expand, and began to pull together people from other countries to provide investment capital. In this way he could help to rebuild the country by funding development of the garment industry, which is now one of the biggest employers. In 2008 Khay completed a PhD in law, and is still always on the lookout for an opportunity. He bought a house in Phnom Penh to use as a base and now spends much of his time there. Khay spent time as an advisor to the Cambodian government on issues of international law and Thai/Cambodia border affairs, but then joined the Royal Cambodian Armed Forces and has risen to the rank of Brigadier General.

Mother holds firmly to her Buddhist principles to this day. She has never had a single day of formal education in her life, but she knows its value and instilled that attitude into her children. Mother spends almost none of her money on herself, but instead uses it to fund the building of temples and schools in regional areas of Cambodia. She pays teachers salaries so that poor children can attend classes, and arranges for wells to be drilled so that villages can have access to clean water. Mother believes in Karma; that acts committed in the present life will affect her future lives. In 2007 she was diagnosed with breast cancer and faced both the disease and its treatment with the same matter-of-fact dignity that has carried her throughout her life. Thankfully her Karma seems to be in positive balance and her disease has been in remission for some time now. Mother regularly visits Cambodia, just to keep an eye on things.

Angkar's leader, *Bong Ti Muoy,* 'Brother Number One', remained in hiding near the Thai border while the Vietnamese army drove the Khmer Rouge from power. He lived out the remainder of his life in obscurity and died in 1998 at the age of seventy-three. It was far better than he deserved.

To this day Dana always has enough food in her house to last a month, and is still unable to throw away anything edible.

It took twenty years, but she eventually got over her aversion to pumpkin and sweet potatoes.

Dana kept the umbrella that she brought from Thailand until it finally fell apart.

She is still terrified of leeches.

Front L-R, Mei (10), Mother, Father, Veng (10). Back L-R, Huor, Khay (15), Dana (13), Keang, her husband Peng. Phnom Penh, Cambodia, 1980.

Dana Hui Lim was born in Cambodia and was only six years old when the Pol Pot regime seized power. She survived the rule of the Khmer Rouge through a combination of good luck, and a determination to survive that she had not previously known she possessed.

Dana arrived in Australia when she was eighteen years old. She was unable to speak English and had virtually no formal education. She began high school in Year Ten, went on to complete a university degree and began a career in the Australian Public Service.

Dana wants to share her story with others to encourage them to persevere in the face of adversity. She would also like to urge her countrymen to discuss their experiences, or set down their own stories so that they are not lost forever. Her book serves as a warning to people of all nations and races, to be wary of the danger than can occur when ideology is not subjected to reason.

CPSIA information can be obtained at www.ICGtesting.com
Printed in the USA
LVOW01s2042170714

394816LV00024B/962/P